庄子语录

QUOTATIONS FROM ZHUANGZI

白话整理　菅咏梅

英文翻译　管晓霞

山东友谊出版社

Shandong Friendship Publishing House

BOOKS OF QUOTATIONS FROM ANCIENT CHINESE PHILOSOPHERS

目录
Contents

庄子语录·目录

Contents

一 仁义道德
Benevolence and morality

1. 至人无己，神人无功，圣人无名。《庄子·逍遥游》

【白话】 道德修养高尚的"至人"能够达到忘我的境界，精神超脱物外的"神人"心目中没有功名利禄，思想修养完美的"圣人"从不追求名誉和地位。

【英译】 The perfect man cares for no self; the holy man cares for no merits; the sage cares for no fame.

2. 无为为之之谓天，无为言之之谓德，爱人利物之谓仁，不同同之之谓大，行不崖异之谓宽，有万不同之谓富。《庄子·天地》

【白话】　　用无为的态度去处世就是道，用无为的态度去表达就是德，给人以爱、给物以利就是仁，能包容不同就是大，行为不标新立异就是宽容，能包罗万象就是富有。

【英译】　To act by doing nothing is called the way of the heaven; to speak by saying nothing is called virtue; to love people and benefit things is called humanity; to tolerate differences is called greatness; to behave without ostentation is called generosity; to embrace varieties of things is called wealth.

3. 彼至正者，不失其性命之情。《庄子·骈拇》

【白话】　　那所谓的至理正道，就是不违背自然所赋予的事物的本性。

【英译】　　The so-called proper way is not to deviate from the essence of the inborn nature and the predestined fate.

4. 今世之仁人，蒿目而忧世之患；不仁之人，决性命之情而饕贵富。《庄子·骈拇》

【白话】　如今世上的仁人，放目远望而忧虑人间的祸患；那些不仁的人，摒弃人的本真和自然而贪求富贵。

【英译】　Nowadays, the humane look at the disorderly society with sad eyes; the inhumane abandon the essence of their inborn nature to seek after honor and wealth.

5. 天下莫不以物易其性矣。小人则以身殉利，士则以身殉名，大夫则以身殉家，圣人则以身殉天下。《庄子·骈拇》

【白话】　天下没有谁不因为外物而改变自身的本性。平民百姓为了私利而牺牲自己，士人为了名声而牺牲自己，大夫为了家族而牺牲自己，圣人则为了天下而牺牲自己。

【英译】 Everyone in the world has been affected by external things and thus has changed his inborn nature. The common people sacrifice themselves for the sake of personal gains; the scholars sacrifice themselves for the sake of fame; the officials sacrifice themselves for the sake of the family; the sages sacrifice themselves for the sake of the state.

6. 吾所谓臧者，非所谓仁义之谓也，任其性命之情而已矣。《庄子·骈拇》

【白话】 我所说的完善，绝不是所谓的仁义，只是放任天性、保持真情罢了。

【英译】 What I would call perfect is not the so-called humanity and justice, but the indulgence of the inborn nature and maintenance of true feelings.

7. 虽以天下誉之，得其所谓，謷然不顾；

以天下非之，失其所谓，傥然不受。天下之非誉，无益损焉，是谓全德之人哉！
《庄子·天地》

【白话】 即使天下的人都称誉他，称誉的言词合乎他的德行，他也傲然不顾；即使让天下人都非议他，使他丧失了名声，他也无动于衷，不予理睬。天下人的非议和赞誉，对于他没有任何的影响，这就是德行完备的人啊！

【英译】 Even if everyone in the world praises him and agrees with what he has done, he will not care; even if everyone in the world condemns him and disgraces what he has done, he will not care. The praise and condemnation of the people in the world cannot affect him. This is the man of perfect virtue.

8. 知穷之有命，知通之有时，临大难而不惧者，圣人之勇也。《庄子·秋水》

【白话】 知道困顿是因为命运，知道通

达是由于时势，面临大难而不畏惧，这就是圣人之勇。

【英译】 To know that misfortune is because of destiny and fortune is because of luck, not to show fear in front of great trouble—these manifest the courage of the sages.

9．不以心捐道，不以人助天，是之谓真人。《庄子·大宗师》

【白话】 不用心智去损害大道，也不用人为的因素去辅助自然，这就叫"真人"。

【英译】 Never impair Tao with the mind and never assist heaven with human efforts. This is what the true man was like.

10．圣人法天贵真，不拘于俗。《庄子·渔父》

【白话】 圣人总是效法自然看重本真，不受世俗的拘束。

【英译】　The sage always follows nature, cherishes simplicity and is free of worldly strains.

11. 今世俗之君子，多危身弃生以殉物，岂不悲哉。《庄子·让王》

【白话】　现在世俗所谓的君子，大多危害身体、弃置生命而一味地追逐身外之物，这难道不可悲吗？

【英译】　Nowadays the so-called gentlemen in the earthly world have endangered their health and sacrificed their lives in pursuit of external things. Isn't it lamentable?

12. 自事其心者，哀乐不易施乎前，知其不可奈何而安之若命，德之至也。《庄子·人间世》

【白话】　注重自我修养的人，悲哀和欢乐都不容易使他受到影响，知道世事艰难、无可奈何却又能安于命运、顺应自然，这就是道德修养的最高境界。

【英译】 The cultivated person is not vulnerable to sadness and happiness. He is contented with his destiny by knowing the hardship of life and follows the natural law. This is the perfection of virtue.

13. 达生之情者, 不务生之所无以为; 达命之情者, 不务知之所无奈何。《庄子·达生》

【白话】 通晓生命真正意义的人, 不会去追求生命所不必要的东西; 洞悉命运之理的人, 不会去追求命运无可奈何的事情。

【英译】 Those who understand the essence of life do not seek after what is beyond the reach of life; those who understand the essence of destiny do not seek after what is beyond the power of destiny.

14. 同则无好也，化则无常也，而果其贤乎！《庄子·大宗师》

【白话】　与万物同一就没有偏私，顺应变化就不固执，你果真成了贤人啊！

【英译】　When you are in harmony with everything on earth, you will have no partiality. When you are in accordance with the changes in the world, you will be free from obstinacy. Then you will be a real sage.

15. 夫欲免为形者，莫如弃世。弃世则无累，无累则正平，正平则与彼更生，更生则几矣。《庄子·达生》

【白话】　想要免于为形体劳累的人，不如舍弃俗世。舍弃俗世就没有劳苦，没有劳苦就心平气和，心平气和就能和自然一起变化更新，跟自然一起变化更新也就接近于大道了。

【英译】　He who wants to get rid of

physical labor had better abandon earthly affairs. Without earthly affairs, there will be no physical labor. Without physical labor, he will be able to keep a peaceful mind. With the peaceful mind, he will be able to evolve with nature. Being able to evolve with nature, he will be able to get close to Tao.

16. 是以圣人和之以是非而休乎天钧,是之谓两行。《庄子·齐物论》

【白话】 古代圣人不执著于是非的争论,保持事物的自然均衡,这就叫"两行"。

【英译】 The ancient sages reconciled right and wrong, thus enjoying a peaceful and harmonious life. That is called the principle of "live and let live".

17. 夫大道不称,大辩不言,大仁不仁,大廉不嗛,大勇不忮。《庄子·齐物论》

【白话】 真正的道是无法说明的,最了

不起的辩说是不用言说的，真正的仁爱是不必向人表示仁爱的，真正的廉洁是不必表示谦让的，真正的勇敢是从不伤害他人的。

【英译】 The true Tao goes beyond description; the true argument goes beyond words; the true humaneness goes beyond benefaction; the true probity goes beyond modesty; the true courage goes beyond violence.

18. 夫道不欲杂，杂则多，多则扰，扰则忧，忧而不救。《庄子·人间世》

【白话】 推行大道不宜繁杂，繁杂了就多事，多事就会受到烦扰，烦扰就引起忧患，忧患到来时就不可挽救了。

【英译】 In publicizing Tao, you should avoid being complicated, otherwise there may be excessive matters to attend to, and the excessive matters may cause disturbance, and disturbance will lead to suffering, and then the case will be helpless.

19. 德荡乎名，知出乎争。名也者，相轧也；知也者，争之器也。《庄子·人间世》

【白话】 道德的失真在于追求名声，智慧的外露在于争强好胜。名声是人们互相倾轧的根源，智慧是人们互相争斗的工具。

【英译】 Virtue is spoiled for the sake of pursuing fame; wisdom is displayed for the sake of contention. Fame is the source of discordance; wisdom is the tool of contention.

20. 夫事其亲者，不择地而安之，孝之至也；夫事其君者，不择事而安之，忠之盛也。《庄子·人间世》

【白话】 侍奉双亲的人，无论何时何地都要使父母安适，这是孝心的最高表现；

侍奉国君的人，无论办什么事都要让国君放心，这是最大的尽忠。

【英译】 Therefore, to wait upon one's parents and make them feel at ease everywhere is the perfection of filial piety. To serve one's ruler and make him feel reassured in every situation is the perfection of loyalty.

21. 死生亦大矣，而无变乎己，况爵禄乎！《庄子·田子方》

【白话】 死与生也算得上是大事了，却不能使圣人有什么改变，更何况爵位与俸禄呢？

【英译】 Life and death, important as they are, could not affect the sages. Let alone rank and stipend!

22. 贵富显严名利六者，勃志也。容动色理气意六者，谬心也。《庄子·庚桑楚》

【白话】 高贵、富有、尊显、威严、声

名、利禄六项，是扰乱意志的因素。容貌、举止、美色、情理、辞气、意志六项，是束缚心灵的因素。

【英译】 Eminence, wealth, distinction, prestige, fame and profit are the six elements that disturb your will. Appearances, manners, beauty, reason, temperament and attitudes are the six elements that bind your heart.

23. 恶欲喜怒哀乐六者，累德也。去就取与知能六者，塞道也。《庄子·庚桑楚》

【白话】 憎恶、欲念、欣喜、愤怒、悲哀、欢乐六项，是牵累道德的因素。去舍、依从、贪取、施与、智虑、技能六项，是堵塞大道的因素。

【英译】 Hatred, desire, joy, anger, sorrow and happiness are the six elements that are the burdens of virtue. Rejection, compliance, greed, dispensation, intelligence and skill are six elements that are the obstacles to Tao.

24. 礼者，世俗之所为也；真者，所以
受于天也，自然不可易也。《庄子·渔父》

【白话】 礼仪，是世俗人的行为；纯真，
却是禀受于自然，出自自然因而也就不
可改变。

【英译】 Following the rituals is the con-
duct of the worldly man; purity and in-
nocence is the natural disposition, and
accordingly not changeable.

25. 以德分人谓之圣，以财分人谓之贤。
《庄子·徐无鬼》

【白话】 能用道德去感化他人的人称作
圣人，能用财物去周济他人的人称作贤
人。

【英译】 He who shares his virtue with
others is called a sage and he who
shares his property with others is called
a worthy man.

15

26. 古之真人，以天待人，不以人入天。

《庄子·徐无鬼》

【白话】 古时候的真人，用顺其自然的态度对待人事，不会用人事干扰自然。

【英译】 The true men in ancient times dealt with earthly affairs with a natural attitude and never disturbed nature with earthly affairs.

27. 至礼有不人，至义不物，至知不谋，至仁无亲，至信辟金。《庄子·庚桑楚》

【白话】 最好的礼仪是没有人我之分，最好的道义是没有物我之分，最高的智慧是不用谋略，最大的仁爱是不分亲疏，最大的诚信是不用金钱作凭证。

【英译】 The best ritual is to have no distinction between self and others; the best righteousness is to have no distinction between self and things; the highest intelligence is not to use schemes; the greatest love is not to be expressed; the greatest faithfulness is not to use money as credence.

28. 此皆就其利，辞其害，而天下称贤焉。《庄子·盗跖》

【白话】 （尧、舜、善卷、许由）这些人都能选取对他们有利的东西，舍弃对他们有害的东西，因而普天下的人们称赞他们是贤明的人。

【英译】 They took what was good for them and rejected what was bad for them. Therefore, they are considered as men of virtue and intelligence by people in the world.

29. 天下大器也，而不以易生，此有道者之所以异乎俗者也。《庄子·让王》

【白话】 天下是最为贵重的了，可是却不用它来换取生命，这就是有道之人对待天下跟世俗人大不一样的地方。

【英译】 The Throne is the most valuable in the world, but it should not substitute life. This is the difference between the people endowed with Tao and the earthly people in their attitude towards power.

30. 孝子不谀其亲，忠臣不谄其君，臣子之盛也。《庄子·天地》

【白话】 孝子不奉承他的父母，忠臣不谄媚他的国君，这是忠臣、孝子尽忠尽孝的极点。

【英译】 A filial son does not fawn upon his parents and a loyal minister does not flatter his lord. This is the best for the loyal ministers and filial sons.

31. 通于天下者，德也；行于万物者，道也；上治人者，事也；能有所艺者，技也。《庄子·天地》

【白话】 贯穿于天地的是顺应自然的

"德"；通行于万物的是听任自然的"道"；善于治理天下的是各尽其能各任其事；能够让能力和才干充分发挥的是各种技巧。

【英译】 What links the heaven and the earth is virtue; what acts upon everything in the world is Tao; what makes the state well governed is administrative duties; what brings ability and talents into full play is skill.

32. 天下有道，则与物皆昌；天下无道，则修德就闲；千岁厌世，去而上仙；乘彼白云，至于帝乡。《庄子·天地》

【白话】 天下太平，圣人就跟万物一同昌盛；天下纷乱，圣人就修身闲居；活了千岁而厌恶活在世上，便离开人世上天成仙；乘着他的白云，去到天帝居住的地方。

19

【英译】 When Tao prevails in the world, the sage will prosper together with everything in the world; when Tao stops prevailing in the world, the sage will cultivate his morality and live a reclusive life. When he is fed up with life after living in the world for a thousand years, he will leave the world and go to the heaven as an immortal. He will go by the white cloud to the place where the heavenly king lives.

33. 古之真人，不知说生，不知恶死；其出不䜣，其入不距；翛然而往，翛然而来而已矣。《庄子·大宗师》

【白话】 古时候的"真人"，不懂得喜欢生存，也不懂得厌恶死亡；出生不欣喜，入死不推辞；无拘无束地走开，自由自在地归来罢了。

【英译】 The true man in ancient times knew neither the joy of life nor the sorrow of death. He was not elated when he was born; he was not reluctant when

he died. Lightheartedly he went away
and lightheartedly he came back.

34. 其生若浮，其死若休。《庄子·刻意》

【白话】　圣人活着犹如在水面漂浮，死
亡犹如疲劳后的休息。

【英译】　For the sage, life is like float-
ing on the water and death is like a rest.

35. 圣人之生也天行，其死也物化。《庄
子·刻意》

【白话】　圣人活着是顺应自然而行，死
后与万物化为一体。

【英译】　The sage follows nature when
he is alive and unites with everything in
the world when he is dead.

36. 古之真人，得之也生，失之也死；得
之也死，失之也生。《庄子·徐无鬼》

【白话】　古时候的真人，得失听其自然，
以得为生，以失为死，以得为死，以失

为生。

【英译】 For the true men in ancient times, some thought that life was gain and death was loss while others thought that death was gain and life was loss.

37. 古之至人，先存诸己而后存诸人。所存于己者未定，何暇至于暴人之所行！《庄子·人间世》

【白话】 古时候道德修养高尚的至人，总是先保全自己才去扶助他人。如果不能保全自己，哪里还有时间阻止暴君的暴行呢！

【英译】 The men of perfect virtue in ancient times always took care of themselves before they helped the others. If they cannot even take care of themselves, how can they hold back the tyrant?

38. 忘其肝胆，遗其耳目，芒然彷徨乎

尘垢之外，逍遥乎无事之业，是谓为而不恃，长而不宰。《庄子·达生》

【白话】　圣人忘却了自己的肝胆，遗忘了自己的耳目，无心地徘徊于世俗之外，自由地生活在不求功业的环境中，这就叫做有所作为而不自恃其功，有所建树而不主宰。

【英译】　The sage forgets his liver and gall and neglects his eyes and ears. He wanders beyond the earthly world aimlessly. He lives in the world of inaction freely. This is called working without taking credit, making accomplishments without being arrogant.

39. 德人者，居无思，行无虑，不藏是非美恶。四海之内共利之之谓悦，共给之之谓安。《庄子·天地》

【白话】　有德行的人安居时不思索，行动时不谋划，不计较是非美丑。与天下人共同分享利益就感到喜悦，共同施予就感到安乐。

【英译】　The man of virtue does not
contemplate when he has settled down;
he does not design when he takes
actions; he does not care about the distinction of right and wrong, or good and
evil. To share the benefit with the others in the world is joy for him and to give
is his happiness.

40. 众人役役, 圣人愚芚, 参万岁而一成
纯。《庄子·齐物论》

【白话】　人们都忙忙碌碌, 圣人却好像
十分愚昧无所觉察, 他糅合古往今来的
许多变化, 自身却浑然一体, 不为外界
的纷乱所困扰。

【英译】　The common people hustle and
bustle while the sage seems to be dull
and ignorant, blending the changes
through time into uniformity without being confused by the imbroglio outside.

41. 圣人并包天地，泽及天下，而不知其谁氏。是故生无爵，死无谥，实不聚，名不立，此之谓大人。《庄子·徐无鬼》

【白话】 圣人包容天地，恩泽施及天下，而百姓却不知道他是谁。因此他生前没有爵禄，死后没有谥号，财物不曾汇聚，名声不曾树立，这才是伟大的人。

【英译】 The sage embraces the heaven and the earth, and bestows his graces all around the world, but the people do not know who he is. Therefore, he does not hold office when he is alive; he does not receive posthumous titles when he is dead; he does not accumulate wealth and he does not establish fame. He can be called a great man.

25

42. 圣人不从事于务，不就利，不违害，不喜求，不缘道；无谓有谓，有谓无谓，而游乎尘垢之外。《庄子·齐物论》

【白话】　圣人不从事那些世俗的事务，不追逐私利，不回避灾害，不喜好贪求，不拘泥于道；没说话又好像说了，说了话又好像没有说，而心神遨游于尘俗世界之外。

【英译】　The sage is never involved in worldly affairs. He does not try to seek after benefits or avoid harms; he does not take delight in seeking after or blindly clinging to Tao. He says nothing and seems to have said something; he says something and seems to have said nothing. Thus, his soul is able to travel beyond the earthly world.

43. 夫至德之世，同与禽兽居，族与万物并。恶乎知君子小人哉！同乎无知，其德不离；同乎无欲，是谓素朴。素朴而民性得矣。《庄子·马蹄》

【白话】　在人性最完善的时代，人与鸟兽共同生存，与万物共同生长，不分君子小人。大家都不用智巧，因而人的本性不会丧失；大家都没有私欲，所以都纯真质朴。纯真质朴才能使人民保存天性。

【英译】 In the times of perfect virtue, human beings live together with birds, animals, and everything in the world. There is no distinction between the inferior man and the superior man. Everyone is ignorant and will not lose the virtue. Everyone is free from desires and in a state of simplicity, which will maintain the inborn nature of the people.

44. 屈折礼乐,呴俞仁义,以慰天下之心者,此失其常然也。《庄子·骈拇》

【白话】 用礼乐去规范和纠正人民的言行，用仁义去抚慰感化天下的人民，这样做便使人民失去人的常态。

【英译】 To regulate and rectify the behavior of the people with ritual and music, and to comfort and influence the people with humanity and justice will make the people lose the normal natural state.

45.不忘其所始,不求其所终。受而喜之,忘而复之,是之谓不以心捐道,不以人助天。《庄子·大宗师》

【白话】 圣人不忘记自己的本原,也不寻求自己的归宿,事情来了就欣然接受,忘掉生死让其复归自然,这就叫做不用心智去损害大道,也不用人为的因素去辅助自然。

【英译】 The sage does not forget the origin of his life and does not explore the final destiny of his life. He is pleased to accept what comes into his life and to forget life and death and just let it be. This is what is meant by not impairing Tao with the mind and not assisting the heaven with human efforts.

46. 故执德之谓纪，德成之谓立，循于道之谓备，不以物挫志之谓完。《庄子·天地》

【白话】 所以保持德行就是有纲纪，德行的实践就是有建树，遵循大道就是完备，不因外物而损害心志就是完人。

【英译】 Therefore, to persevere in virtue is the principle; to perform virtue is achievement; to follow Tao is completion; not to be affected by external things is perfection.

47. 若夫不刻意而高，无仁义而修，无功名而治，无江海而闲，不道引而寿，无不忘也，无不有也，澹然无极，而众美从之。此天地之道，圣人之德也。《庄子·刻意》

29

【白话】 如果不刻意追求而品德高尚，不讲仁义而能修身，不求功名而能治世，不隐居江湖而能悠闲自得，不加保养而能长寿，无所不忘，无所不有，恬淡宁静而将所有的美集于一身，这才是天地的大道，圣人的德行。

【英译】 If we can be lofty without painstaking pursuit, self-cultivated without caring about humanity and justice, governing well without pursuing honor and fame, living leisurely without reclusion and enjoying a long life without health maintenance, we can forget everything yet possess everything; we can enjoy serenity and assemble all forms of beauty. This is the great Tao of heaven and earth and the virtue of the sages.

48. 夫恬淡寂寞虚无无为，此天地之本而道德之质也。《庄子·刻意》

【白话】 恬淡、寂寞、虚无、无为，这便是天地的本原和道德的本质。

【英译】 Indifference, solitude, emptiness and inaction, these are the source

of the heaven and earth and the essence of virtue.

49. 夫遇长不敬, 失礼也; 见贤不尊, 不
仁也。《庄子·渔父》

【白话】 遇到年长者不尊敬是失礼, 见
到贤能者不尊敬是不仁。

【英译】 It is impolite not to show cour-
tesy to elders and it is inhuman not to
show respect to a man of wisdom.

50. 故德有所长, 而形有所忘。《庄子·
德充符》

【白话】 所以只要有过人的德行, 形体
上的残疾就会被人们遗忘。

【英译】 Therefore, for a man with perfect virtue, his physical defects would
be forgotten by the others.

二 为人处世

Attitude towards life

1. 大巧若拙。《庄子·胠箧》

【白话】 最大的智巧就好像是笨拙一样。

【英译】 The great wisdom seems awkward.

2. 传其常情，无传其溢言，则几乎全。《庄子·人间世》

【白话】 传达人之常情，不要传达过分的话语，那么也就大概可以保全自己了。

【英译】 Convey the truth and never convey the exaggerated words, and then you can protect yourself from harm.

3. 凡事亦然：始乎谅，常卒乎鄙；其作

始也简，其将毕也必巨。《庄子·人间世》

【白话】 无论什么事情都是这样：开始时相互谅解，到后来往往互相欺诈；开始的时候很单纯，到后来就变得很复杂。

【英译】 This is truth of all things: they may begin with mutual understanding but end up with mutual deceiving; begin with simplicity but end with complexity.

4. 夫两喜必多溢美之言，两怒必多溢恶之言。《庄子·人间世》

【白话】 双方十分亲近，就肯定有很多过分称颂的言词；双方十分仇视，就肯定有很多过分贬低的言词。

【英译】 When the two are pleasant to each other, there must be an excess of exaggerated compliments; when the two are resentful to each other, there must be an excess of exaggerated rebukes.

5. 唇竭而齿寒。《庄子·胠箧》

【白话】 嘴唇没了牙齿就会外露受寒。

【英译】 Since the lips are gone, the teeth get cold.

6. 真者，精诚之至也。不精不诚，不能动人。《庄子·渔父》

【白话】 本真是精诚的极点。不精不诚，就不能感动人。

【英译】 The natural disposition is the acme of sincerity. Without sincerity, you will never be able to affect the others.

7. 君子之交淡若水，小人之交甘若醴。君子淡以亲，小人甘以绝。《庄子·山木》

【白话】 君子之间的交情清淡得像水一样，小人之间的交情甘美得像甜酒一样。君子间的交情虽然清淡但是亲切，小人间的交情虽然甘甜却容易断绝。

【英译】 The relationship between the

superior men is as plain as water; the relationship between the inferior men is as luscious as wine. The former is plain but close while the latter is luscious but callous.

8. 桂可食，故伐之；漆可用，故割之。人皆知有用之用，而莫知无用之用也。《庄子·人间世》

【白话】 桂树因为可以吃而遭到砍伐，漆树因为可以用而遭到刀割。人们都知道有用的用处，却不知道无用的用处。

【英译】 Cinnamon is edible, and so the trees that yield it are cut down; varnish is useful, and so the trees that produce it are slashed. Everyone knows the benefit of being useful, but does not know the benefit of being useless.

9. 凡外重者内拙。《庄子·达生》

【白话】 凡是对外物看得过重的人，其

内心一定笨拙。

【英译】 Those who pay more attention to external things are clumsy internally.

10．无入而藏，无出而阳，柴立其中央。三者若得，其名必集。《庄子·达生》

【白话】 不要进入荒山野岭把自己深藏起来，也不要进入世俗使自己处处显露，要像木头一样处于出入之间。如果能做到这三点，肯定会得到最高的名声。

【英译】 Do not conceal yourself in the barren mountains or show yourself in the earthly world. You should stay in the middle like a piece of wood. If you can achieve this, you will get the highest honor.

11．知命不能规乎其前，丘以是日徂。《庄子·田子方》

【白话】 孔子说："知道命运是不可预测的，所以我只是每天随着自然的变化而变化、前进。"

【英译】 Confucius said, "Knowing I cannot foretell my fate, I just go on from day to day."

12. 其动止也，其死生也，其废起也，此又非其所以也。《庄子·天地》

【白话】 运动、静止、死亡、生存、衰废、兴盛，这六种情况全都是出于自然而不知其所以然的事情。

【英译】 Movement and stillness, life and death, ups and downs are all natural but beyond reasoning.

13. 大块载我以形，劳我以生，佚我以老，息我以死。《庄子·大宗师》

【白话】 大地给予我形体，给我生命来使我劳苦，用衰老来使我清闲，用死亡来使我安息。

【英译】 The great earth endows me with my physical form, makes me toil

with life, gives me ease with old age and
let me rest with death.

14. 故善吾生者，乃所以善吾死也。《庄子·大宗师》

【白话】 所以把生命看做好事的，也应该把死亡看做好事。

【英译】 Therefore, to live is something good and to die is also something good.

15. 死生，命也，其有夜旦之常，天也。人之有所不得与，皆物之情也。《庄子·大宗师》

【白话】 死和生都是天命，就像黑夜和白天交替那样永恒地变化，完全出于自然。有些事情是人力所不能干预的，这都是事物的常情。

【英译】 Life and death are destined, just like the eternal succession of day and night, which is a natural course of events. These things are beyond the power of human beings. This is true of everything in the world.

16. 且夫得者，时也；失者，顺也；安时而处顺，哀乐不能入也。《庄子·大宗师》

【白话】 至于生命的获得，是因为适时；生命的丧失，是因为顺应自然。能够安于天时而顺应变化的人，悲哀和欢乐都不会侵入心中。

【英译】 The acquisition of life is in accordance with time and the loss of life is in accordance with nature. Those who are content with whatever happens at the right time and follow the natural course will not be affected by sorrow and joy.

17. 今一以天地为大炉，以造化为大冶，恶乎往而不可哉！《庄子·大宗师》

【白话】 如今把整个天地当做大熔炉，

把造化当做高超的冶炼工匠，用什么方法来安排、冶炼我不可以呢？

【英译】 If I take the heaven and earth as a huge furnace and the creator as a skilled blacksmith, by what means is it right for him to treat me?

18. 以生为附赘悬疣，死为决疣溃痈，夫若然者，又恶知死生先后之所在！《庄子·大宗师》

【白话】 圣人把人的生命看做是气的凝结，像身上的赘瘤一样；把人的死亡看做是气的消散，像毒痈化脓后的溃破一样。像这样的人，又怎么会顾及生死先后的分别呢！

【英译】 The sages see life as the forming of a tumor, and death as the burst of a tumor. How can men like this care about the distinction between life and death!

19. 人之生也，与忧俱生，寿者惛惛，久忧不死，何苦也。《庄子·至乐》

【白话】 人一出生，忧患也就跟着一道产生，长寿的人昏昏沉沉，长久地处于忧患之中而不死去，多么痛苦啊！

【英译】 Human beings are born into the world together with worry and care. The men of longevity are in a confused and depressed situation. They live in worry and care for a long time and do not die. How painful they are!

20. 死生为昼夜。《庄子·至乐》

【白话】 生死就像昼夜一样，属于自然的变化。

【英译】 The succession of life and death is just like the succession of day and night.

21. 生之来不能却，其去不能止。悲夫！
《庄子·达生》

【白话】 生命的到来不能拒绝，生命的离去不能阻止。可悲啊！

【英译】 The coming of life cannot be rejected and the going of life cannot be stopped. Alas!

22. 夫哀莫大于心死，而人死亦次之。《庄子·田子方》

【白话】 最悲哀的莫过于心死，身体的死亡还是次要的。

【英译】 No sorrow is greater than the death of the heart. Even the death of the body is next to it.

23. 死生存亡，穷达贫富，贤与不肖，毁誉，饥渴寒暑，是事之变，命之行也。《庄子·德充符》

【白话】 死、生、存、亡，穷、达、贫、富，贤能与不肖、诋毁与称誉，饥、渴、寒、暑，这些都是事物的变化，都是自然规律的运行。

【英译】 Life and death, gain and loss, failure and success, poverty and wealth, worthiness and worthlessness, praise and blame, hunger and thirst, cold and heat — these are all transformation of things following the natural order.

24. 人生天地之间，若白驹之过隙，忽然而已。《庄子·知北游》

【白话】 人生于天地之间，就像小马在细小的缝隙前一闪而过，只是一瞬间而已。

【英译】 The life of a man is as brief as the passage of a horse through a gap in a wall.

25. 夫以利合者，迫穷祸患害相弃也；以天属者，迫穷祸患害相收也。《庄子·山木》

【白话】 人与人以利益相结合的，遇到困厄、灾祸时就会相互抛弃；以天性相

结合的，遇上困厄、灾祸时就会相互关
照。

【英译】　Those who are related to each
other in terms of profit will abandon each
other in times of poverty and disaster;
those who are related to each other in
terms of nature will take care of each
other in such times.

26. 此木以不材得终其天年。《庄子·山
木》

【白话】　这棵树就是因为不成材而能够
终享天年啊！

【英译】　This tree can live out its natural life span because it is worthless.

27. 为人使易以伪，为天使难以伪。《庄
子·人间世》

【白话】　被他人所驱使就容易作伪，被
天性所驱使就难以作伪。

【英译】　It is easy to put on false appearance when compelled by the others; it is hard to put on false appearance when compelled by nature.

28．汝不知夫螳螂乎？怒其臂以当车辙，不知其不胜任也，是其才之美者也。戒之，慎之！《庄子·人间世》

【白话】 你不知道那螳螂吗？奋力举起它的臂膀去阻挡滚动的车轮，不明白自己的力量不能胜任，这是因为它把自己的才能看得太高的缘故。要警惕，要小心啊！

【英译】 Don't you know the fable of the mantis? The mantis raised its forelegs to stop the rolling wheel, without knowing that is was beyond its power. It is too self-assured. Be cautious and be careful!

29．虎之与人异类而媚养己者，顺也；故其杀者，逆也。《庄子·人间世》

【白话】 老虎与人不同类却驯服于驯养它的人，是因为养老虎的人能顺着它的性子。所以那些遭到伤害的人，是因为触犯了老虎的性子。

【英译】 The tiger is of different species from man, yet it is tamed to its keeper because the keeper complies with its dispositions. The tiger get murderous only when it is irritated.

30. 古之所谓隐士者，非伏其身而弗见也，非闭其言而不出也，非藏其知而不发也，时命大谬也。《庄子·缮性》

【白话】 古时候的所谓隐士，并不是隐居而不见人，并不是缄默不言不吐露真情，也不是深藏才智不表露看法，是因为世运背离了天道啊。

【英译】 The so-called hermits in ancient times did not hide themselves away from the others, did not remain silent and conceal the truth, did not conceal their wisdom and opinions. It is all because that they were living in adverse times.

31. 当时命而大行乎天下，则反一无迹；不当时命而大穷乎天下，则深根宁极而待，此存身之道也。《庄子·缮性》

【白话】 一旦行时走运大行于天下，就会返归至精粹纯一境界而不显露踪迹。一旦时运不济而穷困潦倒，就闭口不言来等待时运的变化。这就是保全自身的方法。

【英译】 When times are favorable and they can do great deeds, they will conceal themselves by resorting to Tao; when times are unfavorable and they become down and out, they will keep silent and wait for the turn of fortune. This is the way of self-preservation.

32. 忠谏不听，蹲循勿争。《庄子·至乐》

【白话】　忠诚的劝谏不被君主接纳，那就退让一旁不要再去谏争了。

【英译】　If your loyal suggestions are not accepted by the lord, you should step aside and do not argue any more.

33．名止于实，义设于适。《庄子·至乐》

【白话】　名实要符合，义理的设定要适应各自的天性。

【英译】　The reputation should be in accordance with the reality and principles should be in accordance with individuality.

34．直木先伐，甘井先竭。《庄子·山木》

【白话】　长得很直的树木总是先被砍伐，甘甜的井水总是先被汲干。

【英译】　The trees that are straight get cut down firstly; the wells that are sweet get drawn dry firstly.

35．彼无故以合者，则无故以离。《庄子·山木》

【白话】 凡是无缘无故结合在一起的，也就会无缘无故地离散。

【英译】 Those who get related to each other for no reason will get separated with no reason.

36．入其俗，从其令。《庄子·山木》

【白话】 每到一个地方，就要遵从当地的风俗、政令。

【英译】 Wherever you go, follow the local customs and laws.

37．乐未毕也，哀又继之。哀乐之来，吾不能御，其去弗能止。《庄子·知北游》

【白话】 欢乐还未消逝，悲哀又接着到来。悲哀与欢乐的到来，我无法阻挡；悲哀与欢乐的离去，我也不可能制止。

【英译】 Before the joy is over, sorrow comes in succession. I can neither pre-

49

vent joy and sorrow from coming, nor
can I prevent them from going.

38．草食之兽不疾易薮，水生之虫不疾
易水，行小变而不失其大常也，喜怒哀
乐不入于胸次。《庄子·田子方》

【白话】 吃草的兽类不怕变换草泽，水
生的虫类不怕改变池沼，这是因为只有
小的变化而没有失去根本的生存条件，
这样喜怒哀乐的情绪就不会进入内心。

【英译】 Animals that feed on grass do
not mind the change of swamps; insects
living in the water do not mind the
change of ponds. This is because that
minor changes do not affect the basic
living conditions. Thus, feelings like joy,
anger and sorrow will not affect them in
the least.

39．鹄不日浴而白，乌不日黔而黑。黑
白之朴，不足以为辩。《庄子·天运》

【白话】　天鹅不是天天洗才白,乌鸦不是日日染才黑。黑白都是天然生成的,不必辩论。

【英译】　The swans are white not because they bathe themselves everyday; the crows are black not because they dye themselves everyday. They are born white or black and there is no need for argumentation.

40. 天地非不广且大也,人之所用容足耳。《庄子·外物》

【白话】　天地不能说不宽广,但人所用的只是容身之地而已。

【英译】　Although the heaven and the earth are vast and broad, what we need is a place where you can put your feet.

41. 以瓦注者巧,以钩注者惮,以黄金注者惽。其巧一也,而有所矜,则重外也。《庄子·达生》

【白话】 用瓦片作为赌注的人便心神自在，用金属带钩作赌注的人便心里恐惧，用黄金作赌注的人便心智昏乱。赌博的技巧本来是一样的，有所顾惜，是因为过于重视外物呀。

【英译】 Those who make a bet with tiles are at ease; those who make a bet with a metal hook are worried; those who make a bet with a piece of gold are in confusion. Gambling skills are similar. You have scruples because you think much of the external things.

42. 美成在久，恶成不及改，可不慎与！

《庄子·人间世》

【白话】 成就一件好事需要很长时间，做出一件坏事就后悔莫及、难以补救了，为人处世能不谨慎吗？

【英译】 To accomplish something good takes a long time, while once you do something wrong, it may be too late to amend. You cannot be too careful!

43. 察乎安危，宁于福祸，谨于去就，莫
之能害也。《庄子·秋水》

【白话】　善于观察情况的安危，对于幸
福和灾祸都能内心平静，无论舍弃还是
获取都很谨慎，所以没有什么能伤害他。

【英译】　　He is good at observing fortune and misfortune, not disturbed by
whatever comes to him and prudent in
making decisions of abandoning or
taking. Therefore, nothing can do harm
to him.

44. 其马力竭矣，而犹求焉，故曰败。《庄
子·达生》

【白话】　马已经筋疲力尽了，还要它奔
跑，所以说它会倒下。

【英译】　The horse was exhausted, but
he kept it galloping. That is why I said
they would fall.

45. 先圣不一而能，不同其事。《庄子·至乐》

【白话】 古代的圣贤不企求人们有统一的才能，也不企求人们做相同的事情。

【英译】 The ancient sages did not hope that all the people had the same talent or did the same thing.

46. 且有大觉而后知此其大梦也，而愚者自以为觉，窃窃然知之。《庄子·齐物论》

【白话】 只有非常清醒觉悟的人才能知道人生就像一场大梦，可愚笨的人却以为自己是清醒的，以为自己明察一切，什么都知道。

【英译】 Only the one who is completely awakened can realize that the life is just like a grand dream, while the fool thinks that he is awake and aware of everything.

47. 势为天子而不以贵骄人，富有天下
而不以财戏人。《庄子·盗跖》

【白话】 权势高贵为天子，也不应该因
为地位高贵而轻视别人，一个人富有天
下，也不能以自己的财富戏弄别人。

【英译】 Some people may be as powerful as kings, but they will not despise
the others because of their positions.
Some people may possess as much as
a kingdom, but they will not be domi-
neering because of their wealth.

48. 时雨降矣，而犹浸灌；其于泽也，不
亦劳乎？《庄子·逍遥游》

【白话】 及时雨已经降了，可是还在不
停地浇水灌地；这对于滋润禾苗而言，
不显得徒劳吗？

【英译】 If you continue to water the
fields when timely rains have fallen, isn't
it a waste of labor?

49．且子独不闻夫寿陵余子之学行于邯郸与？未得国能，又失其故行矣，直匍匐而归耳。《庄子·秋水》

【白话】 你难道没听过寿陵少年去邯郸学步的事吗？他没学到赵国人走路的技巧，反而忘了自己走路的方法，以至于只能爬着回家。

【英译】 Haven't you heard of the story that a young man from Shouling went to Handan to learn their way of walking? He failed to learn how to walk as the people in Handan and forgot his own way of walking. As a result, he had to crawl home.

50．处势不便，未足以逞其能也。《庄子·山木》

【白话】 处在不利的情势下，就不能充分施展才能。

【英译】 When a person is in an unfavorable situation, he cannot bring his competence into full play.

51. 好面誉人者, 亦好背而毁之。《庄子·盗跖》

【白话】 好当面夸奖别人的人, 也好背地里诋毁别人。

【英译】 Those who praise somebody to his face are likely to smear him behind his back.

52. 施于人而不忘, 非天布也。《庄子·列御寇》

【白话】 给予别人恩惠却总忘不了让人回报, 这远不是自然对天下广泛而无私的赐予。

【英译】 Doing a favor for the others with the intention of receiving rewards is not a favor at all.

53. 凡人心险于山川, 难于知天。《庄子·

57

列御寇》

【白话】 人心比山川还要险恶，了解人心比预测天象还要困难。

【英译】 The human mind is more tricky than steep cliffs. Understanding the human mind is more difficult than predicting the weather.

54. 功成之美，无一其迹矣。事亲以适，不论所以矣；饮酒以乐，不选其具矣；处丧以哀，无问其礼矣。《庄子·渔父》

【白话】 功业的成就在于完美，不必拘于一定的途径。侍奉双亲是为了让他们感到安适，不必考虑为什么；饮酒是为了欢乐，没有必要选择酒菜和餐具；居丧是为了表达哀伤，不必讲究规范和礼仪。

【英译】 The end justifies the means, so there are various ways of achieving the purpose. Waiting on the parents is to make them feel comfortable and there is no need to worry about the means. Drinking is for happiness and there is no need to care about the dishes and tableware. Holding a funeral is to express the grief and there is no need to pay attention to rituals.

55. 天地之养一也，登高不可以为长，居下不可以为短。《庄子·徐无鬼》

【白话】　天地养育万物是一视同仁的，登上了高位不可自以为尊贵，身处低下的地位也不可自以为卑贱。

【英译】　The heaven and earth provide the same nourishment to everything in the world. There is nothing to be proud of for being in the high position and there is no need to feel inferior for being in the low position.

56. 戒之哉！嗟乎！无以汝色骄人哉！《庄子·徐无鬼》

【白话】 警惕啊！千万不要用高傲的态度对待别人啊！

【英译】 Take it as a warning! Never treat the others arrogantly!

57. 狗不以善吠为良，人不以善言为贤。
《庄子·徐无鬼》

【白话】 狗不因为能叫便是好狗，人不因为会说话便是贤能的人。

【英译】 A dog is not considered good merely because it barks well and a man is not considered virtuous because he speaks well.

58. 鸟兽不厌高，鱼鳖不厌深。夫全其形生之人，藏其身也，不厌深眇而已矣。
《庄子·庚桑楚》

【白话】 鸟兽不满足高飞，鱼鳖不满足水深。那些保全身体和本性的人要隐藏自己，也是不满足深幽高远罢了。

【英译】 Therefore, the birds and beasts

do not mind how high the mountain is and the fish and turtles do not mind how deep the water is. Those who want to remain safe and conceal themselves do not mind how remote and reclusive they live.

59. 不能容人者无亲，无亲者尽人。《庄子·庚桑楚》

【白话】 不能容人的人没有人亲近，没有人亲近的人也就为人们所弃绝。

【英译】 He who cannot tolerate the others will have no friend close to him. He who has no friend close to him will be abandoned by the others.

60. 昔予为禾，耕而卤莽之，则其实亦卤莽而报予；芸而灭裂之，其实亦灭裂而报予。《庄子·则阳》

【白话】 从前我种庄稼，耕地时轻率马虎，粮食的收成就不好；锄草时轻率马虎，而粮食的收成也就很微薄。

【英译】 I used to plough the fields in a
rash way and the yield was not good; I
used to weed in a rash way and the yield
was bad.

61．势为天子，未必贵也；穷为匹夫，未
必贱也。贵贱之分，在行之美恶。《庄子·
盗跖》

【白话】 权势大如天子，未必尊贵；穷
困为贫民，未必卑贱。贵贱的分别在于
品行的美恶好坏。

【英译】 Someone as powerful as the
king may not be noble and superior, and
someone as poor as a pauper may not
be humble and inferior. The distinction
of nobility and humbleness lies in the
virtue.

62．生有为，死也。劝公，以其死也，有
自也；而生阳也，无自也。《庄子·寓言》

【白话】　活着追逐外物、恣意妄为，便要走向死亡。劝诫人们，人的死亡是有原因的；而好好活着，就要无为，无为当然是没有来由的。

【英译】　Reckless actions lead to death. Remember that man dies for some reason or other. If you want to keep on living, you should take no actions and without actions, there will be no reason.

63.剞核大至，则必有不肖之心应之。《庄子·人间世》

【白话】　大凡过分苛责别人的人，那么肯定会使别人产生不好的念头来对付他。

【英译】　When men are pushed too far, they are bound to brood revenge.

64.骐骥骅骝，一日而驰千里，捕鼠不如狸狌，言殊技也。《庄子·秋水》

【白话】　好马一天可以奔驰上千里，捉老鼠却不如狸猫与黄鼠狼，这是说技能不一样。

【英译】 A good horse can gallop a thousand li a day but cannot equal a cat or a weasel in catching mice. This is to say that everyone has different expertise.

65. 以富为是者，不能让禄；以显为是者，不能让名；亲权者，不能与人柄。《庄子·天运》

【白话】 以财富为追求对象的人，不会让给别人利禄；以名声为追求对象的人，不会让给别人名誉；迷恋权势的人，不会授人权柄。

【英译】 Those who pursue wealth will not give up fortune to the others; those who pursue reputation will not give up fame to the others; those who pursue power will not give up positions to the others.

66. 泉涸，鱼相与处于陆，相呴以湿，相濡

以沫,不如相忘于江湖。《庄子·天运》

【白话】　泉水干涸了,鱼儿相互依偎在陆地上,靠大口出气来取得一点儿湿气,靠唾沫来相互润湿,却不如在江湖里彼此相忘。

【英译】　When the springs dry up, the fish are stranded on the land, moistening each other with their breath and damping each other with their slime. But it would be much better for them to live in the rivers or lakes and forget each other.

67. 今且有人于此,以随侯之珠弹千仞之雀,世必笑之,是何也?则其所用者重而所要者轻也。《庄子·让王》

【白话】　现在如果有这样的人,用珍贵的随侯宝珠去打飞得很高的麻雀,世人一定嘲笑他,为什么呢?因为他所用的东西很贵重而要得到的东西却很轻微。

【英译】　Nowadays, if there is a man

who uses a precious pearl to shoot at a flying sparrow, he will be surely laughed at. Why? It is because he is paying such a high price for an insignificant gain.

68. 以人之言而遗我粟，至其罪我也又且以人之言。《庄子·让王》

【白话】　当权者因为别人的话而派人赠予我米粟，将来他也会因为听信别人的话而加罪于我。

【英译】　The lord ordered his men to send me grain because of what the others told him. One day he may lay crimes on me because of what the others told him.

69. 鹪鹩巢于深林，不过一枝；偃鼠饮河，不过满腹。《庄子·逍遥游》

【白话】　小鸟在森林中筑巢，不过占用一根树枝；偃鼠到大河边饮水，不过喝满肚子。

【英译】 The wren that builds a nest in the deep forest occupies only a single branch; the mole that drinks from the river takes only a bellyful.

70. 泽雉十步一啄,百步一饮,不蕲畜乎樊中。神虽王,不善也。《庄子·养生主》

【白话】 沼泽边的野鸡走上十步才能啄到一口食物, 走上一百步才能喝到一口水, 可是它丝毫也不希望被养在笼子里。生活在笼子里虽然安逸, 但它并不自在。

【英译】 The marsh pheasant has to walk ten steps to find a peck of food and a hundred steps for a peck of drink, but it does not want to be raised in a cage. Even though it might live well in the cage, it would not feel comfortable.

71. 平为福, 有余为害者, 物莫不然, 而财其甚。《庄子·盗跖》

【白话】 拥有的东西达到平均水平是福

气，有余就是祸害，凡是事物没有不是这样的，而财物尤其突出。

【英译】 Average possession means happiness; surplus means trouble. This applies to all and it is even so with material acquisition.

72. 灾人者，人必反灾之。《庄子·人间世》

【白话】 加害别人的人，别人必定反过来害他。

【英译】 Those who do harmful things to the others will be harmed by someone else in turn.

73. 自伐者无功；功成者堕，名成者亏。《庄子·山木》

【白话】 自己夸耀的人反而没有功绩；功业成功而不知退隐的人必定会毁败，名声彰显而不知韬光养晦的人必定会遭到损伤。

【英译】 He who is conceited will not accomplish anything; he who does not retire after his accomplishment will come to ruin; he who rests on his fame will suffer from losses.

74. 为不善乎显明之中者，人得而诛之；为不善乎幽间之中者，鬼得而诛之。明乎人，明乎鬼者，然后能独行。《庄子·庚桑楚》

【白话】 明目张胆地作恶，便要受到大众的制裁；暗地里作恶，就要受到鬼神的制裁。能够坦然面对人，坦然面对鬼神的人，就能独行而无愧。

【英译】 He who does evils overtly will be condemned by the others; he who does evils covertly will be condemned by his conscience. He who can face the others and his conscience with an easy mind will be able to go alone without fear.

75. 荣辱立，然后睹所病；货财聚，然后睹所争。《庄子·则阳》

【白话】 世间有了荣辱的区别，各种弊端就显示出来了；财货日渐聚积，然后各种争斗就表露出来了。

【英译】 When honor and disgrace is well defined, malpractices came into being; when wealth is accumulated, disputes began to appear.

76. 德溢乎名，名溢乎暴，谋稽乎诿，知出乎争，柴生乎守，官事果乎众宜。《庄子·外物》

【白话】 德行的败坏由于追求名声，名声的败坏在于张扬，谋略生于危急，机智出于斗争，闭塞是由于固执，官府事务的处理要顺应民意。

【英译】 Virtue overflows for the sake of fame; fame overflows for the sake of showing off; schemes arise from emergency; quick wits arise from disputes; ignorance arises from obstinacy; government affairs should be conducted in accordance with the will of the people.

77. 天下有道，圣人成焉；天下无道，圣人生焉。《庄子·人间世》

【白话】　　天下有道，圣人可以成就事业；天下无道，圣人只能保全性命。

【英译】　When Tao prevails in the world, the sage will be able to succeed; when Tao does not prevail in the world, the sage can only preserve his own life.

78. 可乎可，不可乎不可。道行之而成，物谓之而然。《庄子·齐物论》

【白话】　世界上可以做的事情有可以做的理由，不可以做的事情有不可以做的理由。道路是人们走出来的，事物的名字是人们叫出来的。

【英译】　There are reasons for doing something and not doing something. A path is formed because we walk on it; a thing has a name because we call it so.

三　修身养性
Self-cultivation

1. 不利货财，不近贵富；不乐寿，不哀天；不荣通，不丑穷。《庄子·天地》

【白话】　不谋财货，不求富贵，不把长寿看做快乐，不把夭折看做悲哀，不把通达看做荣耀，不把穷困看做羞耻。

【英译】　He does not seek property or pursue wealth; he does not regard longevity as happiness or premature death as misfortune; he does not regard high rank as honor or poverty as shame.

2. 无为名尸，无为谋府；无为事任，无为知主。《庄子·应帝王》

【白话】　绝弃求名的心思，绝弃智谋的

策划，绝弃任事的行为，绝弃智巧的思虑。

【英译】 Sever yourself from fame, do away with schemes, shun worldly burdens and give up speculation of wisdom.

3. 至人之用心若镜，不将不迎，应而不藏，故能胜物而不伤。《庄子·应帝王》

【白话】 "至人"的心思就像一面镜子，对于外物的来去不迎不送，如实反映事物本身而无所隐藏，所以能够反映外物而不为外物所损伤。

【英译】 The perfect person has a mind like a mirror, which neither welcomes nor sends things from outside, which reflects things without concealing. Therefore, it can reflect things from outside without getting harmed.

4. 吾所谓聪者，非谓其闻彼也，自闻而

已矣。《庄子·骈拇》

【白话】　我所说的聪敏，不是说能听到别人什么，而是指有自知之明罢了。

【英译】　What I would call keen of hearing is not what can be heard, but self-perception.

5. 吾所谓明者，非谓其见彼也，自见而已矣。《庄子·骈拇》

【白话】　我所说的视觉敏锐，不是说能看见别人什么，而是指能够看清自己罢了。

【英译】　What I would call keen of sight is not what can be seen, but keen insight.

6．古之人，外化而内不化。《庄子·知北游》

【白话】　古时的人，外表变化而内心宁静。

【英译】　People in ancient times may

change outwardly, but not inwardly.

7. 唯至人乃能游于世而不僻，顺人而不失己。《庄子·外物》

【白话】 唯有道德修养极高的至人才能够混迹于世俗而不乖僻，顺随人情却不丧失自我。

【英译】 Only men of perfect virtue can wander in the earthly world without perversity and follow the earthly feelings without losing their personality.

8. 知忘是非，心之适也；不内变，不外从，事会之适也。《庄子·达生》

【白话】 不计较是非，是内心的安适；不改变内心的操守，不顺从外物的影响，遇事就可以顺心应手。

【英译】 You forget about the right and wrong because you have your heart at ease; if you neither change your mind nor follow the influence of external things, you will be at ease with everything.

9. 善养生者，若牧羊然，视其后者而鞭之。《庄子·达生》

【白话】 善于养生的人，就像是放羊一样，看到落后的便使用鞭子赶一赶。

【英译】 Keeping the good heath is just like keeping a flick of sheep — keep whipping the stragglers up.

10. 人之所取畏者，衽席之上，饮食之间，而不知为之戒者，过也。《庄子·达生》

【白话】 人所应该畏惧的，是枕席上的恣意和饮食间的失度，若是不知道有所警戒，实在是过错啊。

【英译】 Debauchery in the bed and at the table is what we should fear. If we fail to take the warning against it, we are in the wrong.

11. 形劳而不休则弊，精用而不已则劳，劳则竭。《庄子·刻意》

【白话】 形体劳累而不休息就会疲乏不堪，精力使用过度而不休息就会元气劳损，劳损就会精力衰竭。

【英译】 If the body is overworked without rest, it will wear out; if the spirit is overworked without refreshment, it will tire out and tiredness will lead to exhaustion.

12. 君将盈耆欲，长好恶，则性命之情病矣。《庄子·徐无鬼》

【白话】 你要是满足嗜好和欲望，增多喜好和憎恶，那么性命的本质就要受损害了。

【英译】 If you satisfy all your desires and yield to all your likes and dislikes, you will do harm to your inborn nature.

中国先贤语录口袋书

13. 为善无近名，为恶无近刑。缘督以为经，可以保身，可以全生，可以养亲，可以尽。《庄子·养生主》

【白话】 做世俗的人所认为的善事，但不要有求名之心；做世俗的人所认为的恶事，但不要受到刑律的惩罚。遵从自然的规律并把它作为养生的准则，就可以保护身体，保全天性，养护精神，就可以终享天年。

【英译】 When you do something good, do not do it for the sake of fame; when you do something bad, do not do it as to incur punishment. If you always act according to the law of nature and stick to it as your principle, you will be able to protect your body, preserve your nature, maintain good health and enjoy a long life.

庄子语录·修身养性

14. 不以好恶内伤其身，常因自然而不益生也。《庄子·德充符》

【白话】 不能以好恶损害自身的本性，经常顺应自然而不人为地给身体、生命增添什么。

【英译】 One should not do harm to his natural qualities by dwelling on what he likes and dislikes. He should always follow the natural course of things, never trying to add anything to his life.

15. 吾以其来不可却也，其去不可止也。吾以为得失之非我也，而无忧色而已矣。
《庄子·田子方》

【白话】 我认为爵禄的到来不能推却，失去也不能阻止。我认为得与失不在于我自身，所以就没有什么可忧愁的了。

【英译】 I think that the granting of honors cannot be rejected and the losing of them cannot be hindered. I think the matter of gaining or losing does not lie in me. Therefore, there is nothing to be worried about.

16. 乐全之谓得志。《庄子·缮性》

【白话】 保持自然的天性就叫做得志。

【英译】 The maintenance of the natural instincts is called happiness and freedom.

17. 名实者，圣人之所不能胜也，而况若乎！《庄子·人间世》

【白话】 名利之心，圣人都很难克服，何况是你呢？

【英译】 Even the sage can hardly resist the temptation of fame, how can you?

18. 古之所谓得志者，非轩冕之谓也，谓其无以益其乐而已矣。《庄子·缮性》

【白话】 古时候所说的得志，并不是指拥有荣华富贵，而是指内心有无以复加的快乐而已。

【英译】 The so-called happiness and

freedom of ancient times does not refer to wealth, but the infinite heartfelt pleasure.

19. 故不为轩冕肆志，不为穷约趋俗，其乐彼与此同，故无忧而已矣。《庄子·缮性》

【白话】 所以不要为了富贵荣华而恣意放纵，也不要因为穷困潦倒而趋附流俗，富贵与穷困一样快乐，所以没有忧虑。

【英译】 Therefore, do not indulge yourself when you are wealthy and do not mix with the vulgar world when you are in poverty. If you can draw the same pleasure from both situations, you will be free from worry and care.

20. 丧己于物，失性于俗者，谓之倒置之民。《庄子·缮性》

【白话】 由于外物而丧失自我，迷失本性于世俗中的人，就叫做本末倒置的人。

【英译】 Those who lose their inborn nature due to external things are men who put the cart before the horse.

21. 形莫若缘, 情莫若率。缘则不离, 率则不劳; 不离不劳, 则不求文以待形, 不求文以待形, 固不待物。《庄子·山木》

【白话】 形体不如顺应自然, 情感不如率真。顺应就不会背离, 率真就不会劳苦; 不背离不劳苦, 就不需要用纹饰来装饰形体, 无须纹饰来装饰形体, 也就不必求于外物了。

【英译】 For your physical form, nothing is better than conformity with nature. For your disposition, nothing is better than sincerity. If you conform to nature, you will not deviate from your nature. If you are sincere, you will not suffer from labor. Thus, there is not need to take special care of your physical form, and then you do not have to depend on ma-

庄子语录·修身养性

terial things.

22. 行贤而去自贤之行，安往而不爱哉！
《庄子·山木》

【白话】 行为良善而除去自我炫耀之心，
到哪里不受到爱戴呢？

【英译】 If you do virtuous things without being self-conceited, where would you go without being loved?

23. 今世之人居高官尊爵者，皆重失之，
见利轻亡其身，岂不惑者！《庄子·让王》

【白话】 现在居于高官显位的人，时时
担忧失去它们，见到利益就不顾自己的
性命，岂不是很糊涂吗？

【英译】 Nowadays, those who are in high positions are worried about losing their positions and sacrifice their lives for profit. Aren't they confused?

24. 能尊生者，虽贵富不以养伤身，虽

贫贱不以利累形。《庄子·让王》

【白话】　能够珍视生命的人，即使富贵也不会贪恋俸禄而伤害身体，即使贫贱也不会因利益而劳累身体。

【英译】　Those who cherish their lives will not seek wealth at the cost of their lives when they are rich and will not seek profit at the cost of their health when they are poor.

25. 知足者不以利自累也，审自得者失之而不惧，行修于内者无位而不怍。《庄子·让王》

【白话】　知足的人不因利禄劳累自己，安闲自得的人遇到损失也不害怕，修养身心的人没有官职也不惭愧。

【英译】　He who is content with what he has will not exhaust himself for profit; he who lives a carefree life will not worry about any loss; he who is self-cultivated will not feel ashamed without an official position.

26. 行乎无名者，唯庸有光。《庄子·庚桑楚》

【白话】 行事不显露名声的人，即使平庸也有光彩。

【英译】 He who acts without caring about fame may be plain but brilliant.

27. 正则静，静则明，明则虚，虚则无为而无不为也。《庄子·庚桑楚》

【白话】 内心平正就会宁静，宁静就会明澈，明澈就会空明，空明就能顺任自然而没有什么做不成的。

【英译】 If you are peaceful in mind, you will enjoy serenity; if you can enjoy serenity, you will be clear in mind; if you are clear in mind, you will enjoy emptiness; if you can enjoy emptiness, you can follow the course of nature and there is nothing you cannot achieve.

28. 知大一，知大阴，知大目，知大均，知大方，知大信，知大定，至矣。《庄子·徐无鬼》

【白话】 一个人知道什么是开始，什么是阴柔，什么是光明，什么是造化，什么是无限，什么是信仰，什么是宁静，那么这个人的造诣就达到极点了。

【英译】 If one knows what is the beginning, what is gentility, what is brilliance, what is transformation, what is infinity, what is belief and what is tranquility, the man has attained the ultimate knowledge.

29. 古之得道者，穷亦乐，通亦乐。所乐非穷通也，道德于此，则穷通为寒暑风雨之序矣。《庄子·让王》

【白话】 古时候得道的人，穷困也快乐，通达也快乐。快乐的原因不在困厄与通达，内心得到了道，人生的穷困和通达就像风雨、寒暑的循序变化了。

【英译】 The men endowed with Tao in ancient times were happy in both favorable and unfavorable situations. The happiness does not lie in the situations. With Tao deeply embedded in mind, the ups and downs in life are just like the changes of wind and rain or winter and summer.

30．养志者忘形，养形者忘利，致道者忘心矣。《庄子·让王》

【白话】 修养心志的人能够忘却形骸，调养形骸的人能够忘却利禄，得道的人能够忘却心机与才智。

【英译】 Therefore, those who seek to cultivate their minds can forget about their physical form; those who seek to preserve their physical form can forget about profits; those who are endowed with Tao can forget about schemes.

31. 乘物以游心，托不得已以养中，至
矣。《庄子·人间世》

【白话】　顺从自然而内心悠游自在，寄
托于不得已而蓄养心中的精气，这就是
人生的最高境界。

【英译】　Set your mind at flight by going along with things as they are, and
cultivate your mind by resigning yourself to the inevitable. That is the perfection of life.

32. 极物之真，能守其本，故外天地，遗
万物，而神未尝有所困也。《庄子·天道》

【白话】　能深究事物的本原，持守事物
的根本，所以忘却天地，忘怀万物，而
精神世界不曾有任何困扰。

【英译】　He is able to explore the source
of everything in the world and sticks to
the essence of everything in the world.
Therefore, he is able to forget about the

heaven and earth, neglect everything in the world and his mind is not disturbed.

33. 宇泰定者，发乎天光。《庄子·庚桑楚》

【白话】　心境安泰镇定的人，就会发出自然的光辉。

【英译】　He who has a peaceful mind radiates with a divine light.

34. 知道者必达于理，达于理者必明于权，明于权者不以物害己。《庄子·秋水》

【白话】　懂得大道的人必定通达事理，通达事理的人必定能随机应变，明白应变的人定然不会因为外物而损伤自己。

【英译】　Those who are aware of Tao are surely able to understand reasoning; those who understand reasoning are surely able to adapt themselves to the situation; those who can adapt themselves to the situation will not get harmed by external things.

35. 巧者劳而知者忧，无能者无所求，饱食而敖游，汎若不系之舟，虚而敖游者也。《庄子·列御寇》

【白话】　机巧的人多劳累，智慧的人多忧虑，不用智巧的人却无所追求，填饱肚子就自由自在地遨游，像没有缆绳的船只一样漂浮在水中，这才是心境空虚而自由遨游的人。

【英译】　Those with skills tire themselves physically; those with wisdom tire themselves mentally. Those without skills or wisdom pursue nothing. With his stomach full, he drifts, like a ship without a cable. Such is the man who wanders freely.

91

36. 圣人安其所安，不安其所不安；众人安其所不安，不安其所安。《庄子·列

御寇》

【白话】　圣人安于自然，却不适应人为的摆布；普通人习惯于人为的摆布，却不安于自然。

【英译】　The sages who are content with the natural state of things are not willing to be ordered about by conscious manipulations; the common people who are accustomed to being ordered about do not feel at ease with the natural state of things.

37. 达生之情者傀，达于知者肖，达大命者随，达小命者遭。《庄子·列御寇》

【白话】　通晓生命实情的人就心胸开阔，精精智巧的人就心境狭小，通达大命的人就顺应自然，精通小命的人就处境不顺。

92

【英译】　Those who know the essence of life are broad-minded; those who are wise and skillful are narrow-minded;

中国先贤语录口袋书

those who understand the secret of longevity follow the course of nature; those
who know that life is relatively short suffer misfortune.

38. 真悲无声而哀，真怒未发而威，真
亲未笑而和。《庄子·渔父》

【白话】 真正的悲痛没有哭声也哀伤，
真正的愤怒没有发作也威严，真正的亲
热不笑也和悦。

【英译】 The true grief is sorrowful even
without wailings; the true anger is sol-
emn even without outbreaks; the true
intimacy is friendly even without smiles.

39. 以目视目，以耳听耳，以心复心。《庄
子·徐无鬼》

【白话】 用眼睛看眼睛所能看见的东西，
用耳朵听耳朵所能听到的声音，用心灵
来关照心灵所能领会的心情。

【英译】 Use your eyes to look at what

can be seen, use your ears to listen to what can be heard and use your heart to comprehend what can be comprehended.

40．不能说其志意，养其寿命者，皆非通道者也。《庄子·盗跖》

【白话】 凡是不能够使自己心境愉快，保养自己寿命的人，都不能算是通达道的人。

【英译】 He who cannot keep his mind in peace or preserve his life cannot be called one endowed with Tao.

41．重生，重生则利轻。《庄子·让王》

【白话】 要看重生命。重视生命就会看轻名利。

【英译】 Cherish your life. If you cherish your life, you will neglect fame and fortune.

42. 至贵，国爵并焉；至富，国财并焉；至愿，名誉并焉。《庄子·天运》

【白话】　最为高贵的，国君的爵位都可以弃之不顾；最为富有的，全国的资财都可以弃之不顾；最为显赫的，任何荣誉都可以弃之不顾。

【英译】　Those who have the most valuable quality of forgetting themselves are willing to discard their titles in a state; those who have the richest wealth of self-contentment are willing to discard the property of a state; those who have the greatest eminence of keeping their inborn nature are willing to discard honors and fame.

43. 逍遥，无为也；苟简，易养也；不贷，无出也。《庄子·天运》

【白话】　自由自在、无拘无束，便是无为；简单朴素就容易养活自己；不支出就不耗费。

【英译】 The freedom of lightheartedness and unconstraint is to do nothing; a life of simplicity is easily fulfilled; if there is no giving, there will be no cost.

44. 乘夫莽眇之鸟，以出六极之外，而游无何有之乡，以处圹埌之野。《庄子·应帝王》

【白话】 神人乘渺茫之鸟飞出天地之外，遨游于虚无之境，徜徉于广阔无垠的旷野。这就是精神的自由。

【英译】 The sage rides on the bird of ease and emptiness, flies out of the universe, wanders in the land of nothingness and stays in the boundless wild field.

45. 明则尘垢不止，止则不明也。久与贤人处则无过。《庄子·德充符》

【白话】 镜子明亮就不沾染灰尘，落上了灰尘也就不会明亮。常和有道德的人相处就没有过错。

【英译】 There is no dust on a bright mirror while a dusty mirror is not bright. If you often stay with a man of virtue, you will be free of faults.

46. 人有修者，乃今有恒；有恒者，人舍之，天助之。《庄子·庚桑楚》

【白话】 人能注重修身，才能培养品德。而品德始终如一的人，就会众望所归，也会得到自然的佑护。

【英译】 He who cultivates himself will have a constant nature; he who has a constant nature is supported by the others and assisted by the heaven.

47. 若能入游其樊而无感其名，入则鸣，不入则止。《庄子·人间世》

【白话】 能悠游于世俗的樊篱之内而不为名利所诱惑，别人能接受你的意见你就说，不能接受你的意见你就不要说。

【英译】　　You can live in the ordinary world but not be affected by the temptation of fame and wealth. If the others take your advice, you can air your view, otherwise, you would better keep silent.

48.纯粹而不杂,静一而不变,惔而无为,动而以天行,此养神之道也。《庄子·刻意》

【白话】　　单纯精粹而不混杂,虚静专一而不变动,恬淡无为,行动顺应自然,这就是养神的道理和方法。

【英译】　　Purity without diversion, concentration without wavering, indifference without action and movement in accordance with nature—these are the essences of spiritual maintenance.

49.饰小说以干县令,其于大达亦远矣。《庄子·外物》

【白话】　　修饰浅薄的言辞以求得高名显

位，那和通晓大道的距离就很远了。

【英译】　Those who seek after fame and rank with petty talk can hardly understand Tao.

50. 行不知所之，居不知所为，与物委蛇而同其波，是卫生之经已。《庄子·庚桑楚》

【白话】　行动时自由自在，安居时无牵无挂，顺应自然，随波同流，这就是养护生命的道理了。

【英译】　To act freely, live without care and follow the course of nature and the main stream — these are the ways of self-maintenance.

51. 故目之于明也殆，耳之于聪也殆，心之于殉也殆。《庄子·徐无鬼》

【白话】　眼睛一味地追求过人的视力就危险，耳朵一味地追求过人的听力就危险，心思一味地追求外物也就危险了。

【英译】　It is dangerous to strain your eyes and strain your ears. It is also dangerous to strain your heart for external things.

52. 缘循、偃佒、困畏不若人，三者俱通达。《庄子·列御寇》

【白话】　顺应自然、顺从人意、懦弱谦下，这三种情况都能遇事通达。

【英译】　To follow the natural development, to submit to the will of the people and to be humble and modest — these three can make things go on well.

53. 汝为知在毫毛，而不知大宁。《庄子·列御寇》

【白话】　（世俗人）把心思用在赐赠酬答等琐碎的小事上，却一点也不懂得宁静、自然和无为。

【英译】　Secular people spend a good

deal of time and energy on trifling matters, but know nothing about serenity and nature.

54. 道与之貌，天与之形，无以好恶内伤其身。《庄子·德充符》

【白话】 道给了人容貌，天给了人形体，不要用好恶来伤害自己的本性。

【英译】 Tao gives man an appearance and the heaven gives man a body. Never do harm to the natural qualities by dwelling on what you like and what you dislike.

【英译】 Therefore, if the man of virtue has to rule the state, the best thing to do is to do nothing. Let the world be and then the people will maintain the inborn nature.

四 无为而治
Governing with inaction

1.故君子不得已而临莅天下,莫若无为。无为也而后安其性命之情。《庄子·在宥》

【白话】 所以,君子不得已而居于统治天下的地位,那就不如无为而治。无为而治才能使人民安居乐业保有自然的天性。

【英译】 Therefore, if the man of virtue has to rule the state, the best thing to do is to do nothing. Let the world be and then the people will maintain the inborn nature.

2. 绝圣弃知而天下大治。《庄子·在宥》

【白话】 弃绝聪明智巧,天下就会得到

治理而太平无事。

【英译】　If we abandon wisdom and intelligence, the world will be well governed and peaceful.

3. 至德之世，不尚贤，不使能；上如标枝，民如野鹿。《庄子·天地》

【白话】　盛德的时代，不标榜贤能，不崇尚技巧；国君如同居于高位，百姓如同野鹿一样无拘无束，自由自在。

【英译】　In the times when virtue prevails, the talented are not honored and skills are not valued. The rulers are as modest as the upper branches of trees and the people are as free as wild deer.

4. 夫天地者，古之所大也，而黄帝尧舜之所共美也。故古之王天下者，奚为哉？天地而已矣。《庄子·天道》

【白话】　天和地，自古以来是最为伟大

的，黄帝、尧、舜都共同赞美它。所以，古时候统治天下的人，做些什么呢？仿效天地罢了。

【英译】 The heaven and the earth are greatly honored since ancient times. They were admired by the Yellow Emperor, Yao and Shun. What have the ancient rulers done? Just follow the examples of the heaven and the earth.

5. 圣人之用兵也，亡国而不失人心。《庄子·大宗师》

【白话】 古代的圣人使用武力，灭掉敌国却不失掉敌国的民心。

【英译】 Therefore, when sage wages a war, he can conquer a state without losing the support of the people.

6. 夫圣人之治，治外乎？正而后行，确乎能其事者而已。《庄子·应帝王》

【白话】 圣人治理天下，是治理外表

吗？圣人先端正自己而后感化他人，确
实让人们各尽所能就是了。

【英译】 When the sage rules the state,
is he ruling over men's external actions?
The sage firstly sets his mind upright
and then influences the others, and he
makes everybody do what they can.

7. 故贵以身于为天下，则可以托天下；
爱以身于为天下，则可以寄天下。《庄子·
在宥》

【白话】 以尊重自身生命甚于尊重天下
的态度治理天下的人，才可以把天下托
付给他；以珍爱自身生命甚于珍爱天下
的态度去治理天下的人，才可以把天下
托付给他。

【英译】 He who treasures his state as
he does his own life can be entrusted
with governing his state; he who loves
his state as he does his own life can be
entrusted with governing his state.

8. 夫民，不难聚也；爱之则亲，利之则至，誉之则劝，致其所恶则散。《庄子·徐无鬼》

【白话】 人民是不难聚集的，爱护他们他们就会亲近，给他们好处他们就会靠拢，给他们奖励他们就会勤勉，给他们所厌恶的东西他们就会离散。

【英译】 The people are not difficult to be assembled. Love them and they will be close to you; benefit them and they will gather around you; reward them and they will work hard; disgust them and they will leave.

9. 庶人有旦暮之业则劝，百工有器械之巧则壮。《庄子·徐无鬼》

【白话】 百姓只要有短暂的工作就会勤勉，工匠只要有器械的技巧就会气壮。

【英译】 The common people will work industriously if they are busy from morn-

ing till night; the artisans will be full of
energy if they are skilled with their tools.

10. 简发而栉，数米而炊，窃窃乎又何
足以济世哉！《庄子·庚桑楚》
【白话】 选择头发梳理，数着米粒下锅，
在这种小事上斤斤计较的人又怎么能够
济世救民呢！
【英译】 Picking the hairs to comb and
counting the grains to cook, how can
people caring for trivial things like this
save the world?

11. 古之君人者，以得为在民，以失为
在己。《庄子·则阳》
【白话】 古代治理国家的人，把功绩归
于百姓，把过失归于自己。
【英译】 The ancient rulers attributed
the success to the people and attributed
the failure to themselves.

12. 以贤临人，未有得人者也；以贤下人，未有不得人者也。《庄子·徐无鬼》

【白话】 以贤人自居而凌驾于他人之上的人，不会获得人们的拥戴；以谦恭待人的人，不会得不到人们的拥戴。

【英译】 Those who lord over the others with their virtue will never get the support of the people; those who condescend over the others will surely win the support of the people.

13. 无以人灭天，无以故灭命，无以得殉名。《庄子·秋水》

【白话】 不要人为毁灭天性，不要用故意的作为去毁灭自然的禀性，不要为获取虚名而不遗余力。

【英译】 Do not destroy the inborn nature deliberately; do not destroy the natural disposition intentionally; do not destroy fame in pursuit of gains.

14. 君子不为苛察。《庄子·天下》

【白话】 君子不对他人求全责备，吹毛求疵。

【英译】 The men of virtue never make excessive demands on the others.

15. 官施而不失其宜，举拔而不失其能，毕见情事而行其所为，行言自为而天下化。《庄子·天地》

【白话】 政府设置官职、发号施令恰到好处，提拔人才不遗漏任何有能力的人，明察人情事理而采取恰当的措施，自己的言行就会感化天下。

【英译】 The government will set up official positions and make orders properly; promote the talented and not miss anyone of ability; investigate and then take proper actions; influence the people in the world with its words and deeds.

109

16. 五官殊职, 君不私, 故国治。《庄子·则阳》

【白话】　各种官员都有自己的职责, 国君不自私, 不偏爱, 国家才能得到治理。

【英译】　Every official has his own duties, the ruler shows no partiality and preference, and then the state will be well governed.

17. 君为政焉, 勿卤莽; 治民焉, 勿灭裂。《庄子·则阳》

【白话】　君主处理政事不要鲁莽, 治理百姓不要轻率。

【英译】　The rulers should not deal with government affairs in a rash way or rule over the people in a rash way.

18. 夫为天下者, 亦奚以异乎牧马者哉! 亦去其害马者而已矣。《庄子·徐无鬼》

【白话】　治理天下, 也跟牧马没有什么不同! 也就是去除害群之马罢了!

【英译】 There is no difference between ruling the state and shepherding. It is no more than getting rid of the black sheep.

19.赏罚利害，五刑之辟，教之末也。《庄子·天道》

【白话】 奖赏处罚，利诱惩戒，施行各种刑法，这是教育失败的表现。

【英译】 The practice of reward and punishment and the operation of laws are representations of poor education.

20.官治其职，人忧其事，乃无所陵。《庄子·渔父》

【白话】 官吏处理好各自的政事，人民安排好各自的事情，就不会出现混乱的情况。

【英译】 If the officials perform their respective duties well and the people arrange their respective affairs well, there will be no trouble.

21. 夫杀人之士民，兼人之土地，以养
吾私与吾神者，其战不知孰善？《庄子·
徐无鬼》

【白话】　杀死他国的士卒和百姓，兼并
他国的土地，用来满足自己的私欲和精
神，这种战争不知有什么好处？

【英译】　I do not know what is the benefit of the war in which you slaughter
the soldiers and the people of the other
country and occupy the land of the other
country to satisfy your personal desire
and spirit.

22. 知者之为，故动以百姓，不违其度，
是以足而不争，无以为故不求。《庄子·
盗跖》

【白话】　睿智的人，总是顺从百姓的心
思行动，不违反民众的意愿。所以，知
足就不会争夺，顺应自然所以不贪求。

【英译】 The men of wisdom act in accordance with the wish of the people and never go against their will. Therefore, the contented do not compete and they act in accordance with nature without greed.

23. 君之所言而然，所行而善，则世俗谓之不肖臣。《庄子·天地》

【白话】 凡是君王所说的就都满口应承，君王所做的就加以奉迎，那就是世俗人所说的不良之臣。

【英译】 To agree with whatever the lord says and praise whatever the lord does is called the disloyal minister by the people.

24. 明王之治，功盖天下而似不自己，化贷万物而民弗恃；有莫举名，使物自喜；立乎不测，而游于无有者也。《庄子·应帝王》

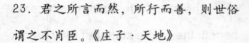

【白话】 圣明的君王治理天下，功盖天下却不归功于自己，教化施及万物而百姓却不觉得有所依赖；功德无量没有什么办法称述赞美，使万事万物各得其所；立足于高深莫测的神妙之境，而处在自然无为的境地。

【英译】 When the enlightened emperor rules the state, his accomplishments benefit the whole state but they do not seem to be out of his efforts; his influence reaches everyone but the people do not feel that they depend on him; his achievements are unfathomable and the people can hardly find words to praise him. He is shrouded in mystery and wanders in the land of nonexistence.

25. 汝游心于淡，合气于漠，顺物自然而无容私焉，而天下治矣。《庄子·应帝王》

【白话】 你神游于恬淡的境界,清静无为,顺应事物自然的本性而没有半点儿个人的偏私,天下就治理好了。

【英译】 Let your mind wander in pure nature, remain inactive, follow the natural courses of events and leave your personal will aside. Thus, the world will be well governed.

26. 闻在宥天下,不闻治天下也。在之也者,恐天下之淫其性也;宥之也者,恐天下之迁其德也。《庄子·在宥》

【白话】 听说过听任天下自由地发展,没听说要治理天下。听任天下自由地发展,是因为担忧人们的本性被扰乱;宽容人们的行为,是因为担忧人们改变了自然的常态。

【英译】 I have heard of letting the world be and letting the world alone, but never heard of governing the world. To let the world be is in fear that the people will

115

go beyond their inborn nature; to let the world alone is in fear that the people will lose their normal state.

27. 故礼义法度者，应时而变者也。《庄子·天运》

【白话】　所以，礼义法度都是顺应时代而有所变化的东西。

【英译】　Therefore, rites and laws are things that change with time.

28. 绝圣弃智，大盗乃止；摘珠毁玉，小盗不起；焚符破玺，而民朴鄙；剖斗折衡，而民不争；殚残天下之圣法，而民始可与论议。《庄子·胠箧》

【白话】　抛弃聪明智巧，才不会出现窃国大盗；毁掉珠玉，才不会发生小偷小摸的事；烧掉契约，砸烂玉玺，人民就淳朴无欲；毁掉度量的器具，人民就不再争夺；毁掉仁义法则，人们才能参与论议。

【英译】 Abandon skill and wisdom, and the robbers will not appear; destroy the pearls and jades, and theft and pilferage will not occur; burn the contracts and crash the seals, and the people will remain simple and unsophisticated; crush the weights and scales, and the people will not quarrel; abolish the laws, and the people will be able to join in the discussion.

29. 彼民有常性，织而衣，耕而食，是谓同德；一而不党，命曰天放。故至德之世，其行填填，其视颠颠。《庄子·马蹄》

【白话】 百姓有他们的本性，织布而后穿衣，耕种而后吃饭，这是共有的本能。人们的思想和行为浑然一体没有一点儿偏私，这叫做任其自然。所以人类天性保留最完善的时代，人们的行动天真笨拙，淳朴而没有心机。

【英译】 The people have their own natural instincts. They weave cloth to get clothes and till the land to get food. This is the common instinct. Their thoughts and actions are the same and there is no partiality. This is in accordance with the nature. Therefore, when the instincts of humans are maintained perfectly intact, people act clumsily and are simple and free from schemes.

30. 是非已明而赏罚次之。《庄子·天道》

【白话】 是非已经搞清楚了，奖赏和惩罚也就不重要了。

【英译】 When right and wrong have been distinguished, reward or punishment is less important.

31. 夫有土者，有大物也。有大物者，不可以物；物而不物，故能物物。《庄子·在宥》

【白话】 拥有国家的，就拥有土地人民。拥有土地人民的，不可以受外物支配；支配外物而不为外物所役使，才能够主宰万物。

【英译】 The one who owns a state owns the land and the people. The one who owns the land and the people should not be influenced by worldly things. Only the one who dominates the world and is not influenced by it can govern everything in the world.

32. 君原于德而成于天。故曰：玄古之君天下，无为也，天德而已矣。《庄子·天地》

【白话】 君主依靠德行来成全自然的本性。所以说：远古的君主治理天下，就是无为而治，顺应自然而已。

【英译】 The ruler regards virtue as the source of his power and heaven as the source of his achievements. Therefore,

庄子语录·无为而治

the ancient rulers ruled over the world
by doing nothing and just followed the
natural course of events.

33. 唯无以天下为者，可以托天下也。《庄
子·让王》

【白话】 只有不以天下为自己所用的人，
才可以把统治天下的重任托付给他。

【英译】 Only he who does not want to
rule over the state can be entrusted with
the throne.

34. 有治在人，忘乎物，忘乎天，其名
为忘己。《庄子·天地》

【白话】 倘若果真存在着什么治理，那
也就是人们遵循本性活动，忘掉外物，忘
掉自然，它的名字就叫做忘掉自己。

【英译】 Governing is to follow the natural instinct of man, if it does exist. To
forget external things and forget nature
is called to forget the self.

五 生活智慧
Wisdom of life

1. 大知闲闲，小知间间。大言炎炎，小言詹詹。《庄子·齐物论》

【白话】 有大才智的人广博豁达，有点小聪明的人则斤斤计较；合于大道的言论气焰凌人，拘于智巧的言论唠叨不休。

【英译】 Men of great wits are open and broad-minded; men of small wits are mean and meticulous. Men in accordance with Tao speak with arrogance; men clinging to ingenuity keep on nagging.

121

2. 日凿一窍，七日而浑沌死。《庄子·应帝王》

五 生活智慧
Wisdom of life

1. 大知闲闲，小知间间。大言炎炎，小言詹詹。《庄子·齐物论》

【白话】 有大才智的人广博豁达，有点小聪明的人则斤斤计较；合于大道的言论气焰凌人，拘于智巧的言论唠叨不休。

【英译】 Men of great wits are open and broad-minded; men of small wits are mean and meticulous. Men in accordance with Tao speak with arrogance; men clinging to ingenuity keep on nagging.

2. 日凿一窍，七日而浑沌死。《庄子·应帝王》

【白话】 每天为混沌凿出一个孔窍，凿了七天混沌就死去了。(混沌是原始纯朴的人民的象征。)

【英译】 They chiseled an aperture everyday and on the seventh day Chaos died. (Chaos stands for the pure ancient people.)

3. 彼其物无穷，而人皆以为有终；彼其物无测，而人皆以为有极。《庄子·在宥》

【白话】 "至道"是没有穷尽的，然而人们却认为有终结；"至道"是不可能探测的，然而人们却认为有极限。

【英译】 The "perfection of Tao" is eternal, while the people consider it ephemeral; the "perfection of Tao" is unfathomable, while the people consider it limited.

4. 吾生也有涯，而知也无涯。以有涯随无涯，殆已；已而为知者，殆而已矣。《庄

子·养生主》

【白话】　人们的生命是有限的，而知识却是无限的。以有限的生命去追求无限的知识，势必非常疲惫。既然这样还要不停地追求知识，只能更加疲惫不堪罢了！

【英译】　Our life is limited, but knowledge is unlimited. To pursue the unlimited knowledge in the limited life is sure to be fatiguing. To know this but still keep on pursuing is even more fatiguing.

5．可以言论者，物之粗也；可以意致者，物之精也。言之所不能论，意之所不能致者，不期精粗焉。《庄子·秋水》

【白话】　可以用言语来谈论的东西，是事物粗浅的表象；可以用心灵来感悟的，则是事物精微的内在本质。既不能用言语谈论，又不能以心意传达的，就不必区分什么精微粗浅了。

【英译】　What can be discussed in

words is something shallow and superficial; what can be felt with heart is something subtle and substantial. For those that can neither be discussed in words nor felt with heart, there is no need to distinguish whether they are shallow or subtle.

6. 小知不及大知，小年不及大年。《庄子·逍遥游》

【白话】　小聪明赶不上大智慧，寿命短的不能了解寿命长的。

【英译】　Little learning does not come up to great learning; the short-lived does not come up to the long-lived.

7. 故大知观于远近。《庄子·秋水》

【白话】　所以具有大智慧的人观察事物从不局限于一个方面、一个部分。

【英译】　Therefore, the man of great intelligence observes things from far and near.

8．大声不入于里耳，折杨、皇荂，则嗑
然而笑。《庄子·天地》

【白话】 高雅的音乐世俗人不可能欣赏，
折杨、皇华之类的民间小曲，世俗人听
了则会欣然而笑。

【英译】 The common people cannot
appreciate grand music, but folk songs
like Zheyang and Huanghua will set
them laughing heartily.

9．是故高言不止于众人之心；至言不出，
俗言胜也。《庄子·天地》

【白话】 所以高雅的言论不可能留在世
俗人的心里；至理名言不能显现，是因
为它被流俗的言论掩盖了。

【英译】 Therefore, the common people
will not keep the lofty speeches in their
minds. The words of truth do not show
themselves because they are covered

125

by the worldly sayings.

10. 六合之外，圣人存而不论；六合之内，圣人论而不议。《庄子·齐物论》

【白话】 天地之外的事，圣人暂且悬置它不加探讨；天地之内的事，圣人只论述它而不加以主观评判。

【英译】 As to what lies beyond the six realms of Heaven and Earth, the sage sets them aside without discussion. As to what lies within the six realms of Heaven and Earth, the sage discusses them but without any subjective comments.

11. 夫知者不言，言者不知，故圣人行不言之教。《庄子·知北游》

【白话】 知道"道"的人不说，说的人并不是真知道"道"，所以圣人施行的是不靠说教的教导。

【英译】 Those who know never say

and those who say never know. Therefore, the sage teaches without words.

12. 圣人者，原天地之美而达万物之理。是故至人无为，大圣不作，观于天地之谓也。《庄子·知北游》

【白话】 圣人探究天地之大美而通达万物的道理。所以至人顺应自然，大圣人不妄自造作，这是说他取法天地的缘故。

【英译】 The sages probe into the beauty of the heaven and the earth to get to know the laws of all things. Therefore, the perfect man follows nature and the great sage does not take any action. This is because that he follows the example of the heaven and the earth.

127

13. 故知止其所不知，至矣；若有不即是者，天钧败之。《庄子·齐物论》

【白话】 知识的探求停止于他所不能知晓的境域，就是极点了；如果不这样，自然的本性就要遭到亏损。

【英译】 It is the acme if the quest for knowledge stops where one does not know; if not so, the natural self will be damaged.

14. 孰知不言之辩，不道之道？若有能知，此之谓天府。《庄子·齐物论》

【白话】 谁能知道不用言说的高论，不用称道的大道？如果有谁能知道，这就叫做圣人的胸怀。

【英译】 Who knows an argument beyond words or Tao beyond description? If a man knows it, he may be called the Reservoir of Heaven.

15. 言者有言，其所言者特未定也。《庄子·齐物论》

【白话】 善辩的人议论纷纭，他们所说

的话也不曾有过定论。

【英译】 The eloquent argue and discuss heatedly, but what they said are not fixed.

16. 道隐于小成，言隐于荣华。《庄子·齐物论》

【白话】 大道被小小的成就所隐蔽，言论被浮华的辞藻所掩盖。

【英译】 Tao is obscured when it is concealed by minor achievements; speech is obscured when it is concealed by flowery words.

17. 欲是其所非而非其所是，则莫若以明。《庄子·齐物论》

【白话】 想要肯定对方所否定的东西而非难对方所肯定的东西，那么不如用澄明的心境去观察事物的本相。

129

【英译】 To approve what the other disapproves and disapprove what the other approves is no better than to observe with a tranquil mind.

18. 知天之所为，知人之所为者，至矣。《庄子·大宗师》

【白话】　知道什么是自然的，知道什么是人为的，这就是智慧的最高境界了。

【英译】　To know what the heaven can do and to know what man can do is the perfection of wisdom.

19. 夫盲者无以与乎眉目颜色之好，瞽者无以与乎青黄黼黻之观。《庄子·大宗师》

【白话】　盲人没法与他观赏眉目和容颜的美丽，也没法跟他共赏彩色锦绣的华美。

【英译】　You cannot appreciate the beauty of a face or the colorful design of a garment with the blind.

20. 古之存身者，不以辩饰知，不以知
穷天下，不以知穷德。《庄子·缮性》

【白话】　古时讲究存身之道的人，不用
辩说来巧饰智慧，不用智慧来困扰天下
人，不用智慧来困扰德行。

【英译】　Those who preserved themselves in ancient times did not ornament
their intelligence with eloquence; they
did not disturb the others with their
intelligence; they did not confuse virtue
with wisdom.

21. 博之不必知，辩之不必慧。《庄子·
知北游》

【白话】　博学的人不一定具有智慧，善
于辩论的人不一定聪明。

【英译】　The well-read man is not necessarily learned; an eloquent man is not
necessarily intelligent.

22. 不知深矣，知之浅矣；弗知内矣，知

之外矣。《庄子·知北游》

【白话】 说不知道的是深奥，说知道的则是浅薄；说不知道的是内行，说知道的才是外行。

【英译】 Ignorance is profound and knowledge is shallow. Ignorance reaches the essence of Tao and knowledge is but superficial.

23．我与若不能相知也，则人固受其黮闇，吾谁使正之？《庄子·齐物论》

【白话】 我们不知道到底什么是对的，什么是错的，而世人都存在偏见，我们又能让谁来评判是非呢？

【英译】 If neither you nor I can tell what is right and what is wrong, the common people will be even more in the dark. To whom should we turn to judge for us?

24．虽有至知，万人谋之。《庄子·外物》

【白话】 一个人虽然有很高的智慧，也怕众人一起打他得主意。

【英译】 Perfect wisdom can be outwitted by ten thousand schemes.

25. 无藏逆于得，无以巧胜人，无以谋胜人，无以战胜人。《庄子·徐无鬼》

【白话】 不要背理贪求，不要用巧诈去战胜别人，不要用谋略去战胜别人，不要用战争去征服别人。

【英译】 Never lust for gains against reason, or conquer the others with deception, scheme or armed forces.

26. 注焉而不满，酌焉而不竭，而不知其所由来，此之谓葆光。《庄子·齐物论》

【白话】 怎么倾注也装不满，怎么汲取也取不尽，而不知其来源，这就叫做隐藏他的光辉。

【英译】 Pour into it and it will never fill; dip from it and it will never dry. You will never know from where it comes. This is called the preserved light.

27. 知与恬交相养，而和理出其性。《庄子·缮性》

【白话】 才智与恬淡的性情相互保养，道德便在心中形成了。

【英译】 When wisdom and tranquility nurture each other, virtue is formed in the heart.

28. 所谓暖姝者，学一先生之言，则暖暖姝姝而私自说也，自以为足矣，而未知未始有物也，是以谓暖姝者也。《庄子·徐无鬼》

【白话】 所谓沾沾自喜的人，就是只懂得了一家之言，就自鸣得意，自以为满足，而不知道自己其实并无所得，这就是沾沾自喜的人。

【英译】 People with smug satisfaction just learn the words from a certain teacher and get satisfied and contented, not knowing that in fact they have not learned anything. Such are the people with smug satisfaction.

29. 知有所困，神有所不及也。《庄子·外物》

【白话】 机智也有困穷的时候，即使神灵也会有始料不及的事情。

【英译】 Wisdom has its limit and even the gods have things beyond their power.

30. 圣人以必不必，故无兵；众人以不必必之，故多兵。《庄子·列御寇》

【白话】 圣哲的人对于必然的事物也不固执，所以总是没有争论；普通人把不是必然的东西看做必然，因而总是争论不休。

【英译】 The sages are not stubborn on the inevitable, so there is no argument;

the common people take the non-inevitable for the inevitable, so there are always arguments.

31. 人之于知也少，虽少，特其所不知而后知天之所谓也。《庄子·徐无鬼》

【白话】 人对于各种事物知道得很少，虽然少，依靠所不知道的而后才能知道自然的大道。

【英译】 Although we only know a little about everything in the world, we can rely on what we have already known to understand nature.

32. 知者之所不知，犹睨也。《庄子·庚桑楚》

【白话】 具有智慧的人也会有不了解的知识，就像斜视一方，所看见的必定有局限。

【英译】 Even those who are intelligent have something that they do not know.

It is just like that what is seen is limited when looking at one side only.

33. 蘧伯玉行年六十而六十化，未尝不始于是之而卒诎之以非也。《庄子·则阳》

【白话】 蘧伯玉活了六十岁，而六十年来与日俱进，往往开始时认为是对的而后来就觉得是错的了。

【英译】 Qu Boyu was sixty years old and learned day by day for sixty years. What he considered right is later considered to be wrong.

34. 人皆尊其知之所知，而莫知恃其知之所不知而后知。《庄子·则阳》

【白话】 人人都重视自己的才智所了解的知识，却不懂得凭借自己所不知道的而后知道别的道理。

【英译】 Everyone knows to cherish what is known with his intelligence, but does not know to get to know what is

35. 是故丘山积卑而为高，江河合水而
为大，大人合并而为公。《庄子·则阳》

【白话】 所以说山丘积聚卑小的土石才
成就其高，江河汇聚细流才成就其大，伟
大的人物并合了众人的意见才成就其公。

【英译】 Therefore, the mountains are
high when the small stones accumulate;
the rivers are large when the small
streams accumulate; the great men are
accomplished when the others' traits
accumulate.

36. 古之人与其不可传也死矣，然则君
之所读者，古人之糟粕已夫！《庄子·天
道》

【白话】 古时候的人跟他们不可言传的
道理一块儿消失了，那么你所读的书，正
是古人的糟粕啊！

【英译】 The people of ancient times

are gone with the truth that they cannot pass on in words. Then what you are reading is all rubbish left over by the ancient people.

37. 三人行而一人惑，所适者犹可致也，惑者少也；二人惑则劳而不至，惑者胜也。《庄子·天地》

【白话】 三个人同行，其中一个人迷路，所要到的地方还是可以到达的，因为迷路的人少；要是两个人迷路就不能到达了，因为迷路的人占多数。

【英译】 When three men walk together and one of them gets confused, they can still reach the destination, because it is just the minority that is confused. If it is two of them who get confused, they can hardly reach the destination, because it is the majority that is confused.

38. 大惑者，终身不解；大愚者，终身

不灵。《庄子·天地》

【白话】 大迷惑的人，终身不能觉悟；大愚昧的人，终身不知道自己愚昧。

【英译】 Those who are in the worst confusion will never get rid of the confusion for their entire lives; those who are the worst fools will never realize it for their entire lives.

39. 井蛙不可以语于海者，拘于虚也；夏虫不可以语于冰者，笃于时也；曲士不可以语于道者，束于教也。《庄子·秋水》

【白话】 井里的青蛙，不可能跟它谈论大海，是因为受到生活空间的限制；夏天的虫子，不可能跟它谈论冰霜，是因为受到时间的限制；乡下的书生，不能和他谈论大道理，是因为他受了礼教的束缚。

【英译】 You cannot talk about the sea with a frog in the well, because it is confined to its dwelling place; you cannot talk about frost with a summer worm, because it is limited to the season; you cannot talk about Tao with a rural scholar, because he is restrained to the rites.

40. 言者所以在意，得意而忘言。《庄子·外物》

【白话】　言语是用来表达真意的，领会了真意就忘掉了言语。

【英译】　Words are used to convey meaning. When the meaning is comprehended, the words are forgotten.

41. 不言则齐，其与言不齐，言与齐不齐也，故曰言无言。《庄子·寓言》

【白话】　没有主观评论，事物的常理自然齐一。原本齐一的常理加上主观的言论就不齐了。既然主观的言论加在自然之理上就不和谐了，所以要说没有主观成见的言论。

【英译】　Without subjective comments,

everything in nature is uniform. With subjective comments, what is uniform becomes not uniform. Therefore, we should speak without subjective comments.

42. 天下皆知求其所不知，而莫知求其所已知者；皆知非其所不善，而莫知非其所已善者，是以大乱。《庄子·胠箧》

【白话】 天下人都知道追求他所不知道的，却不知道探索他所已经知道的；都知道非难他所认为不好的，却不知道否定他所赞同的，因此天下大乱。

【英译】 Therefore, everyone knows to pursue what he knows, but does not know to explore what he has already known; everyone knows to criticize what he dislikes, but does not know to deny what he likes. Thus, the world comes into confusion.

六　道家哲理
Philosophy of Taoism

1. 夫道，覆载万物者也，洋洋乎大哉！君子不可以不刳心焉。《庄子·天地》

【白话】　道，是覆盖万物的，浩瀚广大！君子不可以不抛弃成见去效法大道。

【英译】　Tao covers everything in the world. How magnificent it is! The man of virtue must get rid of the conventions and follow the great Tao.

2. 夫昭昭生于冥冥，有伦生于无形，精神生于道，形体生于精，而万物以形相生。《庄子·知北游》

【白话】　明亮的东西产生于昏暗的东西，有形的东西产生于无形的东西，精神产

庄子语录·道家哲理

143

生于道，形体产生于精气之中，万物都以各种形态互相产生。

【英译】　Brightness originates from darkness, the tangible from the intangible; the spirit from Tao; and the physical form from the spirit. All things are created with their respective forms and shapes.

3. 其与万物接也，至无而供其求，时骋而要其宿；大小、长短、脩远。《庄子·天地》

【白话】　道无时无刻不与万物相联系，虽然它虚无至极，但能适应万物的需要，随时都在变化发展而成为万物的归宿，而且可大可小，可长可短，可近可远。

【英译】　Therefore, Tao is in connection with everything in the world and satisfies the needs of everything in the world, although it is indefinite by itself. It is changing with time to be the dwell-

ing place for everything in the world. It
can be great and small, long and short,
far and near.

4. 道不可有，有不可无。道之为名，所
假而行。《庄子·则阳》

【白话】 道不能执著于有形，也不能执
著于无形。道之所以称作"道"，只不过
是借了"道"的名义而已。

【英译】 Tao does not have a form, but
Tao is not formless. That Tao is called
"Tao" is for the name's sake.

5. 且道者，万物之所由也，庶物失之者
死，得之者生。为事逆之则败，顺之则
成。《庄子·渔父》

【白话】 道是万物产生的根源，各种事
物失去了它，就会死亡，得到了它，就
能生存。做事情顺应了它，就能成功，违
背了它，就会失败。

【英译】 Tao is the source of everything

in the world. Without it, everything in the world will perish. With it, everything will flourish. If we do things in accordance with it, we will succeed. If we go against it, we will fail.

6. 万物职职，皆以无为殖。故曰天地无为而无不为。《庄子·至乐》

【白话】　万物繁多，都从无为的状态中繁殖出来。所以说天地虽然无心作为却又无所不生、无所不为。

【英译】　The varied and numerous things in the world are born with nothing having done anything. Therefore, the saying goes, "The heaven and the earth do nothing and there is nothing they cannot do."

7. 天下有常然。常然者，曲者不以钩，直者不以绳，圆者不以规，方者不以矩，附离不以胶漆，约束不以纆索。《庄子·骈

拇》

【白话】 天下事物都各有它们固有的常态。所谓常态，就是弯曲的不依靠曲尺，笔直的不依靠墨线，圆的不依靠圆规，方的不依靠角尺，使分离的东西附着在一起不依靠胶和漆，将单个的事物捆束在一起不依靠绳索。

【英译】 Everything in the world has its normal state. The so-called normal state is curving without a try square, straight without a ruler, round without compasses, square without an angle square, attached without glue and bound without ropes.

8. 天地与我并生，万物与我为一。《庄子·齐物论》

【白话】 天地与我一起生存，万物与我浑然一体。

【英译】 The heaven and the earth and I exist at the same time; all things in the world and I are one uniformity.

9. 不知周之梦为蝴蝶与，蝴蝶之梦为周
与？《庄子·齐物论》

【白话】 庄子梦见蝴蝶，梦醒后，搞不
清是庄周梦见了蝴蝶呢，还是蝴蝶梦见
了庄周呢？

【英译】 He cannot tell whether it was
Zhuang Zhou dreamed of the butterfly
or the butterfly dreamed of Zhuang
Zhou.

10. 天地一指，万物一马。《庄子·齐物
论》

【白话】 从事理相同的观点来看，天地
只有一种元素，万物纷纷也只是一类。

【英译】 Such is the case with Heaven
and Earth and everything in the world,
they are just like the case with the fin-
ger and the horse——they are the same
substance in nature.

11. 万物一府，死生同状。《庄子·天地》

【白话】　万物最终归结于同一，死与生也并不存在区别。

【英译】　Everything in the world will return to the same root, so there is no distinction between life and death.

12. 指穷于为薪，火传也，不知其尽也。《庄子·养生主》

【白话】　蜡烛有烧尽时候，而火种却世世代代传续下来，永远不会熄灭。

【英译】　The candle may be consumed, but the fire will be passed on, and it will never be extinguished.

13. 物无非彼，物无非是。自彼则不见，自知则知之。故曰：彼出于是，是亦因彼。《庄子·齐物论》

【白话】　各种事物无不存在它自身的对立面，各种事物也无不存在它自身的一面。从他方看就看不到这一面，从自身知道的这一面讲当然是知道的。所以说彼产生于此，此也因此依存于彼。

【英译】 Everything in the world has its otherness and everything in the world has its selfness. What cannot be seen in otherness can be known from selfness. Therefore, otherness comes from selfness and selfness depends on otherness.

14. 方生方死，方死方生；方可方不可，方不可方可，因是因非，因非因是。《庄子·齐物论》

【白话】 各种事物随起随灭，随灭随起，可以的可以变为不可，不可的又可以变为可以，是因非而出现，非因是而产生。

【英译】 Where there is birth there must be death; where there is death there must be birth. Possibility may turn to impossibility and impossibility may turn to possibility. The right may lead to the wrong and the wrong may lead to the right.

15. 天下莫大于秋豪之末，而大山为小。《庄子·齐物论》

【白话】 天下没有什么比秋毫的末端更大，而泰山却是最小的。

【英译】 In the world, there is nothing larger than the tip of the down of the bird and nothing smaller than Mount Tai.

16. 穷则反，终则始；此物之所有。《庄子·则阳》

【白话】 物极必反，结束意味着新的开始，这是事物具有的共同规律。

【英译】 Everything will turn back when it reaches the limit. The end means the beginning. This is the universal law of everything in the world.

17. 非彼无我，非我无所去。《庄子·齐物论》

【白话】　没有对立面就没有我，没有我的对立面我也就无所呈现。

【英译】　There is no otherness if there is no selfness, and if there is no otherness, the selfness cannot show itself.

18. 本在于上，末在于下。《庄子·天道》

【白话】　根本的东西是最重要的，末节的东西则处于不重要的地位。

【英译】　The essence is of extreme importance, while the trivial things are less important.

19. 有天道，有人道。无为而尊者，天道也；有为而累者，人道也。《庄子·在宥》

【白话】　有天道，有人道。无所作为却处于崇高地位的，就是天道；有所作为而劳累困苦的，就是人道。

【英译】 There is the Tao of heaven and Tao of humanity. To do nothing and yet enjoy great honor is the Tao of heaven; to do things and toil is the Tao of humanity.

20. 祸福淳淳，至有所拂者而有所宜。《庄子·则阳》

【白话】 祸福在不停地流转，出现违逆的一面同时也就存在相宜的一面。

【英译】 Fortune and misfortune have their comings and goings. The pros and cons coexist in the same time.

21. 安危相易，祸福相生，缓急相摩，聚散以成。《庄子·则阳》

【白话】 安危相互变易，祸福相互生成，缓急相互交替，聚散因此而形成。

【英译】 Safety and danger alternate with each other; fortune and misfortune interchange with each other; relaxation and emergency succeed each other; accumulation and dispersion are formed like this.

22. 恶乎然？然于然。恶乎不然？不然于不然。《庄子·齐物论》

【白话】 事物为什么是这样的，自然有它是这样的道理；事物为什么不是这样的，自然有它不是这样的道理。

【英译】 When something is like this, there are reasons for it to be like this. When something is not like this, there are reasons for it to be not like this.

23. 是亦彼也，彼亦是也。彼亦一是非，此亦一是非。《庄子·齐物论》

【白话】 此即是彼，彼即是此。彼也有它的是非，此也有它的是非。

【英译】 Selfness is otherness and otherness is selfness. There is right and wrong in otherness and there is right and wrong in selfness.

24. 不以生生死，不以死死生。死生有待邪？皆有所一体。《庄子·知北游》

【白话】 不是为了生才产生死，也不是为了死才终止生。生和死是相辅相成的对立面吗？生和死都是一体的。

【英译】 Death is not generated because of life and life is not stopped because of death. Are life and death opposite to each other? Life and death are closely related.

25. 天无为以之清，地无为以之宁，故两无为相合，万物皆化。《庄子·至乐》

【白话】 天无为而自然清虚，地无为而自然宁静，天与地两个无为相互结合，万物就全都变化生长。

【英译】 The heaven is clear because it does nothing; the earth is quiet because it does nothing. As neither the heaven nor the earth does anything, everything in the world grows and evolves.

26. 天地虽大，其化均也；万物虽多，其治一也；人卒虽众，其主君也。《庄子·天地》

【白话】 天和地虽然很大，它们的演变却是均衡的；万物虽然纷杂，它们的条理却是一致的；百姓虽然众多，他们的主宰却都是国君。

【英译】 Great as they are, heaven and earth evolve in a balanced way; varied as they are, all things in the world follow the same order; numerous as they are, the people have their king as the ruler.

27. 天地者，万物之父母也，合则成体，散则成始。《庄子·达生》

【白话】 天和地，是生养万物的父母，物

质元素结合便形成万物的形态，物质元素一旦离散又成为另一物体产生的开始。

【英译】 The heaven and the earth give birth to everything in the world. Their combination brings the formation of all the things in the world. Their separation brings the beginning of new things.

28. 杂乎芒芴之间，变而有气，气变而有形，形而有生。今又变而之死，是相与为春秋冬夏四时行也。《庄子·至乐》

【白话】 夹杂在若有若无之间，变化而有元气，元气变化而有形体，形体变化而有生命。如今又回到死亡，生死的变化就跟春夏秋冬四季运行一样。

【英译】 Amid what is opaque and obscure, transformation generates vital energy, vital energy generates physical form and physical form generates life. Then it comes back to death. The succession of life and death is just like that of the four seasons.

29. 泽及万世而不为仁，长于上古而不为老，覆载天地刻雕众形而不为巧，此所游已。《庄子·大宗师》

【白话】 泽及万世却不以为仁，比上古还年长却不算老，覆载天地、雕刻出世间所有精巧的形象却不夸耀其技巧，这就是"道"的境界啊！

【英译】 To bestow everlasting favors but not out of humaneness, to enjoy longevity but not to seem old, and to cover the heaven and sustain the earth but not to boast of his skill is the essence of Tao.

30. 杀生者不死，生生者不生。《庄子·大宗师》

【白话】 能够杀死所有生命的主宰者当然不会死，能够产生所有生命的主宰者当然也不存在诞生的问题。

【英译】 The dominator who can take

lives of all the living things will never die. The dominator who can give life to all the living things is not born.

31. 夫物，量无穷，时无止，分无常，终始无故。《庄子·秋水》

【白话】 世界上的事物，数量上是无穷无尽的，时间上是永不停止的，得与失没有一定的规则，终结和起始也没有原因。

【英译】 The things in the world are numerous in number and eternal in time. There are no set rules for gaining and losing and there are no reasons for ending and beginning.

32. 明乎坦途，故生而不说，死而不祸；知终始之不可故也。《庄子·秋水》

【白话】 明白生与死之间犹如一条没有阻隔的平坦大道，因而活着不会倍加欢喜，死亡也不觉得是祸患，这是因为明白了终结和开始是不会一成不变的。

【英译】　Knowing that the difference between life and death is just like a flat road without any obstacles, they neither take life as happiness nor take death as sadness. This is because that there is no fixed point for beginning and ending.

33. 夫天下也者，万物之所一也。得其所一而同焉，则四支百体将为尘垢，而死生终始将为昼夜而莫之能滑，而况得丧祸福之所介乎！《庄子·田子方》

【白话】　天下万物都有共同性。了解他们的共同性而同等看待，那么人的四肢、躯体都可以视为尘垢，生死始终也可以看做昼夜的变化，没有什么能够扰乱内心，更不会在乎祸福得失。

【英译】　Everything in the world has something in common. Get to know the similarities and treat them equally. Then the limbs and bodies of human beings can be taken as dust of the earth. The succession of life and death can be regarded as the succession of day and night. There is nothing that can disturb the peace of mind and the matter of gaining and losing is neglected.

34. 天地有大美而不言，四时有明法而不议，万物有成理而不说。《庄子·知北游》

【白话】 天地具有伟大的美德却不言说，四时有明显的法则却不自己表达，万物变化有永恒的规律却不讲出来。

【英译】 The heaven and the earth have the highest virtue, but they do not speak a single word. The four seasons occur in regular cycles, but they do not raise a single argument. All things in the world change according to a fixed rule, but they do not give a single explanation.

35. 彼为盈虚非盈虚，彼为衰杀非衰杀，彼为本末非本末，彼为积散非积散也。《庄子·知北游》

【白话】 "道"使万物有盈虚而自身却没有盈虚，"道"使万物有衰杀而自身却没有衰杀，"道"使万物有本末而自身却没有本末，"道"使万物有聚散而自身却没有聚散。

【英译】 Tao makes things full or empty, but it is not full or empty; Tao makes things decline and decay, but it is not declining or decaying. Tao makes things begin or end, but it does not begin or end; Tao makes things accumulate or disperse, but it does not accumulate or disperse.

36. 合则离，成则毁，廉则挫，尊则议，有为则亏，贤则谋，不肖则欺，胡可得而必乎哉。《庄子·山木》

【白话】 有聚合就有离散，有成功就有

毁败；锐利就会遭到挫折，尊崇就会遭受议论，有作为就会受亏损，贤能就会被谋算，而无能就会受到欺侮，怎么可以偏滞一方呢！

【英译】 Where there is union there is separation; where there is completion there is destruction; where there is keenness there is frustration; where there is honor there is reproach; where there is accomplishment there is failure; where there is capability, there is undermining; where there is incapability there is bullying. How can we look just at the one side?

37. 道通。其分也成也，其成也毁也。《庄子·庚桑楚》

【白话】 大道通达于万物。任何事物有分离就有新的形成，有形成就有毁灭。

【英译】 Tao permeates through everything. Where there is separation there is formation; where there is formation there is destruction.

38. 同类相从，同声相应，固天之理也。《庄子·渔父》

【白话】 事物同类的就互相聚集，同声的就相互应和，本来就是自然的道理。

【英译】 Things of the same kind cluster and sounds of the same frequency harmonize. This is the law of nature.

39. 人之生，气之聚也；聚则为生，散则为死。若死生之徒，吾又何患！《庄子·知北游》

【白话】 人的诞生，是气的聚合，气的聚合形成生命，气的离散便是死亡。如果死与生是同类相属的，那么对于死亡我又忧患什么呢？

【英译】 The birth of the man is the accumulation of the vital energy. The accumulation of the vital energy forms life and the dispersal of the vital energy leads to death. If life and death are closely related, then why should I worry about death?

40．凡物无成与毁，复通为一。《庄子·齐物论》

【白话】　一切事物从总体来看，没有完成和毁灭，都复归于一个整体。

【英译】　For all the things in the world, there is no construction or destruction and everything belongs to a whole.

41．忘年忘义，振于无竟，故寓诸无竟。《庄子·齐物论》

【白话】　忘掉生死年岁，忘掉是非仁义，遨游于无穷的境地，这样圣人就把自己寄托于无穷无尽的境域之中了。

【英译】　Forget about time, forget about justice, and travel in the realm of the infinite. Thus the sage can repose himself in the realm of the infinite.

42. 因是已，已而不知其然，谓之道。《庄子·齐物论》

【白话】 顺着自然的规律走而不知道为什么这样，这就叫做"道"。

【英译】 To follow the natural course of things without knowing why it is so is called "Tao".

43. 美旁日月，挟宇宙，为其吻合，置其滑涽，以隶相尊。《庄子·齐物论》

【白话】 何不与日月同辉，胸怀宇宙，与万物合为一体，是非混淆而置之不问，把世俗的尊卑贵贱都看做等同。

【英译】 Get close to the sun and the moon and embrace the universe. Thus you will merge yourself with everything in the world so that you can put aside the confusion of right and wrong and treat the superior and inferior equally.

图书在版编目（CIP）数据

庄子语录：英汉对照/王恒展，杨敏主编. —2 版.
—济南：山东友谊出版社，2011.6（2015.4 重印）
（中国先贤语录口袋书）
ISBN 978 – 7 – 80737 – 861 – 7

Ⅰ.①庄… Ⅱ.①王… ②杨… Ⅲ.①英语—汉语—
对照读物 ②庄周（前 369 ~ 前 286）—语录
Ⅳ.①H319.4：B

中国版本图书馆 CIP 数据核字（2011）第 131692 号

中国先贤语录口袋书
庄子语录
主编 王恒展 杨 敏

主　　管：山东出版传媒股份有限公司
集团网址：www.sdpress.com.cn
出版发行：山东友谊出版社
地　　址：济南市英雄山路 189 号　邮政编码：250002
电　　话：出版管理部（0531）82098756
　　　　　市场营销部（0531）82098035（传真）
印　　刷：莱芜市华立印务有限公司
版　　次：2011 年 6 月第 2 版
印　　次：2015 年 4 月第 3 次印刷
规　　格：92mm × 176mm
印　　张：$3\frac{7}{12}$
字　　数：49 千字
定　　价：8.00 元

（如印装质量有问题，请与出版社出版管理部联系调换）